Ecosystem Restoration Strategies: Supporting Climate Change Adaptation, Biodiversity Conservation, Sustainable Development, Natural Capital, Carbon Markets, and Green Economy

Copyright

Ecosystem Restoration Strategies: Supporting Climate Change Adaptation, Biodiversity Conservation, Sustainable Development, Natural Capital, Carbon Markets, and Green Economy

ISBN (eBook): 978-1-991368-35-5

ISBN (Paperback): 978-1-991368-36-2

Published by Global Climate Solutions

First Edition, 2025

Cover design and interior layout by Global Climate Solutions

Table of Contents

Introduction

Ecosystem restoration has become an essential strategy for responding to the growing pressures on natural systems that sustain human life. Forests, wetlands, rivers, oceans, soils, and grasslands provide the foundation for food, water, climate regulation, and biodiversity. Yet these systems are increasingly degraded by human activity, including deforestation, unsustainable agriculture, industrial pollution, and urban expansion. The resulting loss of resilience has weakened ecosystems' ability to absorb shocks and continue supporting livelihoods and economies. Restoration responds to this crisis by actively repairing damaged environments, with the goal of recovering ecological functions and building long-term sustainability.

Restoration differs from conservation in its focus on what has already been lost or degraded. Conservation seeks to preserve what remains intact, while restoration looks forward, using science, policy, and practice to bring back ecosystem health and productivity. Restoration requires deliberate actions, such as reforesting cleared lands, re-wetting drained wetlands, removing barriers in rivers, or rehabilitating degraded soils. These efforts not only restore biodiversity but also strengthen the capacity of ecosystems to withstand climate change, urban growth, and resource demands. By renewing the ecological foundations of human well-being, restoration serves as a pathway to achieving both environmental and development goals.

International initiatives highlight the importance of restoration on a global scale. The United Nations has declared the current decade as the Decade on Ecosystem Restoration, signaling the urgency of reversing decades of degradation. Such initiatives are tied directly to achieving the Sustainable Development Goals, which depend on healthy ecosystems for water security, food production, disaster risk reduction, and climate resilience. Governments, businesses, and communities alike are now acknowledging that ecosystem restoration is not simply desirable but indispensable. A restored environment underpins sustainable economies, strengthens resilience to natural disasters, and helps mitigate greenhouse gas emissions.

Restoration is complex, requiring context-specific approaches informed by ecological science and grounded in social realities. Effective restoration cannot rely solely on technical expertise. It requires governance structures that encourage cooperation, financing mechanisms that support long-term action, and policies that align with broader development objectives. Local knowledge, especially from Indigenous peoples, plays an important role in designing and sustaining restoration practices. At the same time, technological innovations such as remote sensing, artificial intelligence, and digital monitoring provide new tools for assessing progress and scaling interventions.

The challenge ahead is immense. Vast areas of land, freshwater, and marine ecosystems require urgent attention. The costs of inaction are high, including continued biodiversity loss, increasing vulnerability to climate impacts, and declining human well-being. At the same time, the opportunities are significant. Restoration offers the chance to build economies rooted in sustainability, reconnect societies with their natural surroundings, and ensure that future generations inherit a healthier planet. This book explores the principles, strategies, and tools needed to make this vision a reality, providing a comprehensive overview of ecosystem restoration across terrestrial, freshwater, marine, and urban environments, as well as the governance and financing frameworks that support it.

Chapter 1: Foundations of Ecosystem Restoration

Ecosystem restoration begins with a deep understanding of the foundations that shape how natural systems function, why they degrade, and how they can be repaired. It is a discipline that combines ecological science with social, economic, and governance dimensions to restore balance between human activities and the natural world. Laying these foundations requires recognizing ecosystems as complex, interconnected systems that provide essential services for human well-being and planetary stability. By exploring the principles, history, science, and global frameworks underpinning restoration, this chapter establishes the basis upon which effective strategies and practices can be designed and implemented.

Defining Ecosystem Restoration

Ecosystem restoration is the process of assisting the recovery of ecosystems that have been degraded, damaged, or destroyed by human activity or natural disturbances. It involves deliberate and sustained actions to re-establish the structure, function, and resilience of ecosystems, ensuring that they can once again provide essential services to people and nature. Restoration is not simply about recreating what once existed but about enabling ecosystems to regain their capacity to adapt, evolve, and thrive in changing environmental conditions. This includes restoring biodiversity, improving ecological connectivity, and rebuilding the processes that sustain life, such as nutrient cycling, soil formation, water purification, and carbon storage.

The concept of restoration is closely linked to the recognition that ecosystems are dynamic and constantly changing. While it may be possible to aim for a reference state, such as the condition of an ecosystem before significant human disturbance, restoration often focuses on functional outcomes rather than exact historical replication. For example, a restored wetland may not look identical to its pre-disturbance form, but if it provides habitat, improves water quality, and reduces flood risks, it is considered successful. This functional perspective ensures that restoration efforts are relevant to current and future environmental challenges, including climate change and population pressures.

Ecosystem restoration also differs from related approaches such as conservation, rehabilitation, and reclamation. Conservation seeks to maintain existing ecosystems in their current state, preventing further degradation. Rehabilitation involves improving the condition of an ecosystem without fully restoring its original structure or functions. Reclamation typically refers to the conversion of degraded land for specific uses, such as agriculture or development, rather than restoring its ecological integrity. Restoration, by contrast, strives to rebuild ecological systems in ways that restore natural processes and resilience, while often integrating human needs and land-use realities.

One of the key features of ecosystem restoration is its emphasis on ecological integrity and resilience. Ecological integrity refers to the wholeness and functioning of an ecosystem, including its biodiversity, productivity, and capacity to regulate natural cycles. Resilience describes the ability of ecosystems to absorb disturbances and adapt without collapsing into a degraded state. Restoration seeks to enhance both integrity and resilience, ensuring that ecosystems can continue to support human societies in the face of shocks such as extreme weather events, invasive species, or unsustainable exploitation.

The importance of ecosystem restoration lies in the wide range of benefits it delivers. Restored ecosystems provide essential services that underpin human well-being, from clean water and fertile soils to climate regulation and cultural value. They also contribute to global biodiversity goals by creating habitats for species under pressure from habitat loss. Restoration projects can generate social and economic co-benefits, such as new jobs, sustainable livelihoods, and opportunities for education and cultural renewal. By linking ecological health with human development, restoration serves as a bridge between environmental sustainability and social progress.

Defining ecosystem restoration also requires acknowledging the role of people as both drivers of degradation and agents of renewal. Human decisions, policies, and practices have caused widespread ecosystem damage, but they also hold the key to reversing it. Restoration is inherently a collaborative endeavor that requires the involvement of multiple stakeholders, including governments, local communities, businesses, scientists, and civil society. By engaging diverse actors, restoration initiatives can draw on a wide range of knowledge systems, resources, and perspectives to design solutions that are inclusive and sustainable.

Finally, ecosystem restoration must be understood as an ongoing process rather than a one-time intervention. Restoring ecosystems takes time, often spanning decades, as natural systems recover and evolve. Continuous monitoring, adaptive management, and long-term commitment are essential to success. Restoration is as much about stewardship as it is about repair, requiring patience, persistence, and flexibility to respond to changing conditions. It is this process-oriented understanding that makes ecosystem restoration a cornerstone of strategies for achieving sustainable development and resilience in the 21st century.

Historical Perspectives and Evolution of Restoration Practices

The practice of ecosystem restoration has roots that stretch back centuries, even if the term itself is relatively modern. Early societies, often out of necessity, undertook efforts to rehabilitate degraded lands and waters. Traditional agricultural systems in Asia, Africa, and the Americas incorporated practices such as crop rotation, terracing, and managed irrigation to prevent soil erosion and maintain fertility. Indigenous peoples also engaged in ecosystem stewardship, using controlled burns, selective harvesting, and cultural rituals to sustain biodiversity and ensure the regeneration of plants and animals. These early interventions reflected an understanding that human well-being was inseparably tied to healthy ecosystems.

The Industrial Revolution and subsequent waves of agricultural and urban expansion marked a turning point. Rapid exploitation of forests, soils, rivers, and coastal zones fueled economic growth but left behind large-scale degradation. In response, the first organized restoration movements emerged in the late 19th and early 20th centuries. One prominent example was reforestation in Europe, where deforestation had led to soil erosion, flooding, and loss of timber resources. Governments launched large-scale tree planting programs to stabilize landscapes and protect livelihoods. Similarly, in North America, the Dust Bowl of the 1930s spurred soil conservation and land restoration initiatives, such as contour plowing and shelterbelt planting, that aimed to reverse the ecological consequences of poor land management.

The post-war era saw restoration expand into new contexts as scientific understanding of ecology deepened. The rise of ecology as a discipline in the mid-20th century provided a framework for thinking about ecosystems as interconnected systems with complex feedbacks. Restoration became not only a practical response to degradation but also a scientific pursuit. Pioneering restoration projects during this period emphasized re-establishing native vegetation, managing invasive species, and rehabilitating wetlands and rivers. For instance, wetland restoration gained prominence in the United States as awareness grew of their role in flood control and wildlife habitat. These efforts reflected a shift from utilitarian views of ecosystems to a recognition of their intrinsic ecological value.

By the late 20th century, restoration had evolved further, influenced by global environmental movements and growing concern about biodiversity loss and climate change. The 1980s and 1990s marked the institutionalization of restoration ecology as a distinct scientific field. Academic journals, conferences, and professional societies emerged, creating platforms for sharing knowledge and developing standards. International agreements, such as the Convention on

Biological Diversity, recognized restoration as a key strategy for reversing biodiversity decline. During this time, restoration projects became larger in scope, involving whole landscapes and watersheds rather than isolated sites. This reflected a broader understanding that ecological processes operate at multiple scales and that connectivity is vital for resilience.

The early 21st century brought restoration to the forefront of global sustainability agendas. The Millennium Ecosystem Assessment highlighted the extent of ecosystem degradation and its implications for human well-being, reinforcing the urgency of large-scale restoration. The concept of ecosystem services—benefits people derive from nature—helped link restoration to economic and social priorities. Governments and organizations began framing restoration as an investment in natural capital, emphasizing co-benefits such as carbon sequestration, water security, and disaster risk reduction. Advances in technology, including remote sensing, GIS, and ecological modeling, provided new tools for designing, monitoring, and scaling restoration efforts.

The evolution of restoration has also been marked by shifts in philosophy and practice. Earlier approaches often sought to recreate ecosystems as they once were, aiming for historical reference conditions. Over time, the focus has shifted toward restoring functionality and resilience, recognizing that ecosystems are dynamic and that climate change, invasive species, and urbanization make it unrealistic to recreate the past. Restoration now emphasizes adaptive management, integrating ecological science with social and economic considerations. It is seen as both a scientific and a social endeavor, requiring collaboration across disciplines and stakeholders.

Today, restoration is framed as a global imperative. Initiatives such as the UN Decade on Ecosystem Restoration underscore the need for collective action at unprecedented scales. Historical practices, from Indigenous stewardship to early reforestation campaigns, have provided valuable lessons, but contemporary challenges demand new levels of ambition and coordination. The evolution of restoration reflects humanity's growing recognition that repairing ecosystems is not only possible but necessary for building sustainable futures. This trajectory, from traditional land care to global restoration agendas, demonstrates how restoration has matured into a cornerstone of environmental and development strategies worldwide.

The Science of Ecosystem Functions and Processes

Ecosystems are complex networks of living organisms interacting with one another and with their physical environments. The science of ecosystem functions and processes seeks to understand how these systems operate, how they sustain life, and how they respond to disturbances. Ecosystem functions refer to the biological, geochemical, and physical activities within ecosystems, while processes describe the mechanisms that drive these activities. Together, they create the foundation for ecosystem services—the benefits humans derive from nature, such as clean water, fertile soils, pollination, and climate regulation. Understanding these functions and processes is essential for ecosystem restoration because it allows practitioners to design interventions that re-establish ecological balance and resilience.

One of the most fundamental ecosystem processes is energy flow. Through photosynthesis, plants, algae, and certain bacteria capture solar energy and convert it into chemical energy stored in biomass. This energy forms the basis of food webs, supporting herbivores, carnivores, and decomposers. The efficiency of energy transfer between trophic levels shapes ecosystem productivity and determines how much energy is available to sustain different organisms. Disruptions to energy flow, such as the removal of top predators or overharvesting of primary producers, can destabilize food webs and reduce ecosystem resilience. Restoration efforts often seek to reintroduce species or re-establish habitats that stabilize energy flow and food web dynamics.

Nutrient cycling is another critical process. Ecosystems recycle essential elements such as carbon, nitrogen, phosphorus, and water through interconnected biogeochemical cycles. Microorganisms play a central role, breaking down organic matter and releasing nutrients that plants and other organisms can use. For example, nitrogen-fixing bacteria convert atmospheric nitrogen into forms that plants can assimilate, while decomposers return nutrients to soils. Disruptions to nutrient cycles—through pollution, excessive fertilizer use, or habitat degradation—can lead to imbalances, including eutrophication in aquatic systems or soil depletion on land. Restoration projects frequently aim to repair these cycles by enhancing soil health, restoring wetlands, or improving vegetation cover to stabilize nutrient dynamics.

Biodiversity underpins ecosystem functions by providing redundancy and complementarity among species. Redundancy ensures that if one species is lost, others can perform similar ecological roles, while complementarity refers to the way diverse species interact to enhance overall ecosystem performance. For example, different plant species may have varying root depths, which allows ecosystems to capture water and nutrients more efficiently. High biodiversity also increases resilience, enabling ecosystems to recover from disturbances more rapidly. Restoration science emphasizes the re-establishment of native species and habitat diversity as a means to strengthen these processes and maintain functional ecosystems.

Ecosystem regulation processes such as climate moderation, water purification, and disease control further demonstrate the importance of ecosystem functions. Forests regulate local and global climates by sequestering carbon and influencing rainfall patterns. Wetlands filter pollutants and store floodwaters, reducing disaster risks. Grasslands and savannas control the spread of pests and diseases by maintaining predator-prey relationships. When these processes are disrupted, the consequences for human societies can be severe, including increased climate vulnerability, water scarcity, and health risks. Restoration interventions are often designed with these regulatory services in mind, ensuring that ecosystems continue to provide vital benefits to people.

Connectivity between ecosystems is another key consideration. Few ecosystems function in isolation; rather, they are part of larger ecological networks. Rivers link mountains to oceans, transporting sediments and nutrients, while migratory species connect habitats across continents. Fragmentation caused by urban development, infrastructure, or deforestation disrupts these connections, weakening ecological processes. Restoration science emphasizes the importance of ecological corridors, buffer zones, and landscape-level planning to restore connectivity. These interventions not only support wildlife movement but also enhance resilience by allowing ecosystems to function as integrated systems.

Disturbance and succession are natural processes that shape ecosystems. Fires, floods, storms, and volcanic eruptions can cause temporary disruptions but also create opportunities for renewal. Ecological succession refers to the gradual process by which species colonize, establish, and modify environments following a disturbance. Early successional species prepare the ground for later arrivals, leading to more complex and stable communities over time. Understanding these dynamics is crucial for restoration because interventions must account for natural processes of recovery. Sometimes, the best restoration strategy is to remove barriers and allow succession to proceed, while in other cases active interventions are required to guide ecosystems toward desired outcomes.

Human activities have significantly altered ecosystem functions and processes, often accelerating or amplifying natural changes. For example, climate change is shifting temperature and precipitation patterns, disrupting plant growth, migration cycles, and species interactions. Pollution introduces toxic substances into ecosystems, affecting energy flow and nutrient cycling. Overexploitation reduces biodiversity, undermining redundancy and resilience. Restoration science seeks to counteract these impacts by re-establishing processes that can operate sustainably under current and future pressures. This requires adaptive management approaches that recognize uncertainty and adjust strategies as new information emerges.

Technological advances are transforming the study and practice of ecosystem functions and processes. Remote sensing and satellite imagery allow scientists to monitor changes in vegetation, soil moisture, and water quality at large scales. DNA sequencing and environmental genomics reveal the hidden roles of microorganisms in nutrient cycling and ecosystem regulation. Ecological modeling enables predictions about how ecosystems will respond to interventions under different scenarios. These tools provide restoration practitioners with the ability to design more effective, evidence-based strategies that align with natural processes.

Ultimately, the science of ecosystem functions and processes provides the foundation for ecosystem restoration. By understanding how energy flows, nutrients cycle, biodiversity supports resilience, and ecosystems regulate climate and water, practitioners can target interventions that rebuild ecological integrity. Restoration is not about forcing ecosystems into static states but about enabling the dynamic processes that sustain life to function once more. A deep appreciation of ecosystem science ensures that restoration efforts are not only ecologically sound but also socially and economically beneficial, supporting the broader goal of creating sustainable and resilient human-nature systems.

Global Commitments and Frameworks for Restoration

Ecosystem restoration has become a central focus of international environmental policy, with global commitments and frameworks guiding collective action across nations. These commitments recognize that environmental degradation transcends borders and that coordinated efforts are essential to safeguard ecosystems that provide food, water, climate regulation, and biodiversity. The global community has developed agreements, initiatives, and targets that embed restoration into broader agendas of sustainability, climate action, and development. These frameworks not only provide guidance for national strategies but also create accountability mechanisms, ensuring that restoration remains a priority for governments, organizations, and communities worldwide.

The Convention on Biological Diversity (CBD) has been one of the most influential international frameworks advancing restoration. Adopted in 1992, the CBD commits parties to conserve biological diversity, use its components sustainably, and ensure the fair sharing of benefits from genetic resources. Over the years, the CBD has placed increasing emphasis on restoration as a means to achieve its objectives. The Aichi Biodiversity Targets, established under the CBD for the 2011–2020 period, included a specific commitment to restore at least 15 percent of degraded ecosystems by 2020. Although progress fell short of this target, the framework catalyzed global recognition of restoration as a critical component of biodiversity conservation and sustainable development.

The Sustainable Development Goals (SDGs), adopted in 2015 by the United Nations, provide another powerful framework for restoration. Multiple goals are directly linked to the health of ecosystems, including SDG 6 on clean water and sanitation, SDG 13 on climate action, SDG 14 on life below water, and SDG 15 on life on land. Ecosystem restoration is embedded within these goals as a pathway to achieve sustainable resource use, climate resilience, and biodiversity protection. For example, SDG 15.3 explicitly calls for combating desertification, restoring degraded land, and striving to achieve a land degradation–neutral world by 2030. By situating restoration within the SDGs, the international community has tied ecological recovery to the broader agenda of human development and poverty alleviation.

The Paris Agreement on climate change, adopted in 2015, also incorporates restoration through its focus on land use, land-use change, and forestry (LULUCF). Forest restoration and afforestation are recognized as crucial strategies for carbon sequestration and climate mitigation. Countries' nationally determined contributions (NDCs) often include restoration targets, linking ecological recovery with commitments to reduce greenhouse gas emissions. Programs such as REDD+ (Reducing Emissions from Deforestation and Forest Degradation) encourage countries to implement forest restoration as part of global climate goals. In this way, restoration has become an integral element of international climate policy, reflecting its dual role in supporting biodiversity and mitigating climate change.

Several large-scale initiatives and pledges further demonstrate the growing momentum for restoration. The Bonn Challenge, launched in 2011, set a global target to restore 150 million hectares of degraded and deforested land by 2020 and 350 million hectares by 2030. This voluntary initiative has been endorsed by dozens of countries and has inspired regional efforts such as the African Forest Landscape Restoration Initiative (AFR100), which seeks to restore 100 million hectares of land in Africa by 2030. Similarly, the Initiative 20x20 in Latin America and the Caribbean has committed countries to restoring 50 million hectares of degraded land. These efforts highlight how global commitments translate into regional and national action, tailored to local needs and priorities.

The UN Decade on Ecosystem Restoration, declared for the period 2021–2030, represents the most ambitious global effort to date. Coordinated by the UN Environment Programme (UNEP) and the Food and Agriculture Organization (FAO), the initiative calls on all sectors of society to prevent, halt, and reverse ecosystem degradation. The Decade emphasizes scaling up restoration to address the intertwined crises of biodiversity loss, climate change, and human well-being. It promotes knowledge-sharing, capacity-building, and financial support, while encouraging governments, businesses, and communities to integrate restoration into policies and practices. By framing restoration as both a global necessity and an opportunity, the Decade has elevated it to the forefront of international sustainability efforts.

Frameworks for restoration are not limited to environmental agreements but extend into financial and economic domains. Institutions such as the World Bank, Global Environment Facility (GEF), and Green Climate Fund (GCF) support restoration projects that align with broader development and climate objectives. Market-based mechanisms, including carbon credits and payment for ecosystem services, provide incentives for restoration by linking ecological outcomes with economic benefits. These approaches embed restoration within the financial systems that drive global economies, ensuring that ecological recovery is not only an environmental concern but also an investment in long-term prosperity.

At the regional level, organizations and agreements reinforce global frameworks. The European Union, for instance, has adopted biodiversity and restoration strategies that set binding targets for member states, including restoring at least 20 percent of the EU's land and sea areas by 2030. In Africa, the Great Green Wall initiative seeks to restore degraded landscapes across the Sahel region to combat desertification, improve food security, and build resilience to climate change. In Asia, restoration is linked to initiatives for sustainable forestry, watershed management, and disaster risk reduction. These regional frameworks demonstrate how global commitments are adapted to specific ecological and socio-economic contexts.

Civil society and non-governmental organizations play a critical role in advancing global restoration commitments. International NGOs such as the International Union for Conservation of Nature (IUCN) and World Resources Institute (WRI) provide technical expertise, convene stakeholders, and monitor progress toward global targets. Grassroots organizations and community groups implement restoration on the ground, ensuring that global commitments translate into tangible outcomes. Partnerships between governments, businesses, and civil society are increasingly recognized as vital for achieving restoration goals at scale.

The evolution of global commitments and frameworks reflects a growing consensus that restoration is central to addressing the planet's most pressing challenges. These commitments create shared goals, mobilize resources, and provide the accountability needed to sustain long-term action. They link ecological restoration to broader agendas of climate resilience, sustainable development, and human well-being, embedding it into the fabric of international cooperation. By aligning restoration with global priorities, these frameworks establish the foundation for large-scale ecological recovery and sustainable futures.

Chapter 2: Terrestrial Ecosystem Restoration

Terrestrial ecosystems—forests, grasslands, savannas, and soils—form the backbone of life on land, providing food, water regulation, carbon storage, and habitat for countless species. Over centuries, human activities such as deforestation, unsustainable farming, overgrazing, and urban expansion have driven extensive land degradation, reducing the resilience of these ecosystems and undermining their capacity to support societies. Restoration of terrestrial systems is therefore central to global sustainability efforts, reconnecting ecological integrity with human needs. This chapter examines the strategies, practices, and innovations for restoring terrestrial ecosystems, highlighting the pathways through which degraded landscapes can once again thrive.

Forest Restoration and Reforestation Strategies

Forests are among the most biodiverse and productive ecosystems on Earth, providing critical services such as carbon sequestration, water regulation, soil protection, and habitat for countless species. Yet they are also among the most threatened, facing pressures from deforestation, land conversion, illegal logging, wildfires, and climate change. Forest restoration and reforestation strategies aim to reverse these trends by re-establishing forest cover, restoring ecological functions, and ensuring that forests can continue to provide vital ecosystem services. These strategies vary depending on ecological conditions, cultural contexts, and policy frameworks, but they share a common goal: repairing the ecological and social value of forests.

One key approach to forest restoration is natural regeneration, which relies on the capacity of ecosystems to recover when pressures are reduced. By protecting degraded areas from further disturbance, such as grazing or logging, natural processes like seed dispersal and succession can re-establish forest cover. Natural regeneration often produces forests with high biodiversity and resilience, as native species recolonize and ecological processes are restored. However, this approach requires time and supportive conditions, including seed sources and suitable soil quality. Where these conditions exist, natural regeneration can be one of the most cost-effective and ecologically sound strategies.

In areas where natural recovery is unlikely or too slow, active reforestation becomes necessary. Reforestation involves planting trees and shrubs, either of native or carefully selected species, to accelerate forest establishment. Depending on goals, reforestation may prioritize biodiversity, carbon storage, watershed protection, or economic returns. For example, mixed-species plantations can enhance biodiversity and resilience compared to monocultures, while carefully managed production forests can meet timber demands and reduce pressure on natural forests. Success depends on matching species to site conditions, ensuring genetic diversity, and considering long-term ecological interactions.

Another important dimension of forest restoration is agroforestry, which integrates trees into agricultural landscapes. Agroforestry systems provide multiple benefits, including soil enrichment, erosion control, shade for crops, and diversified incomes for farmers. By restoring tree cover in farmlands, agroforestry contributes to both ecological resilience and rural livelihoods. In many regions, agroforestry is recognized as a practical strategy for scaling restoration, as it aligns environmental goals with economic incentives for landholders. Policies and programs that support farmers in adopting agroforestry practices can significantly expand the reach of restoration efforts.

Forest landscape restoration (FLR) has emerged as a comprehensive framework that goes beyond site-level interventions to focus on restoring entire landscapes. FLR emphasizes the integration of ecological, social, and economic objectives, seeking to balance forest restoration with the needs of communities. It acknowledges that restoration does not always mean returning land to pristine forest but may involve mosaics of land uses, including natural forests, plantations, agroforestry, and other productive systems. FLR requires participatory planning, inclusive governance, and long-term monitoring to ensure that restoration benefits both ecosystems and people.

Climate change has added urgency and complexity to forest restoration strategies. Forests play a vital role in sequestering carbon, making reforestation and afforestation important climate mitigation tools. Many countries have included forest restoration in their climate commitments, recognizing its potential to reduce emissions and enhance resilience. However, climate change also poses risks to restoration, as shifting temperatures, altered rainfall patterns, and increased disturbances affect forest dynamics. Successful strategies must therefore incorporate climate adaptation measures, such as selecting climate-resilient species, diversifying plantings, and planning for disturbances like fires and pests.

Policy frameworks and governance systems strongly influence forest restoration outcomes. National and international commitments, such as those made under the Bonn Challenge or the Paris Agreement, provide targets and mobilize resources. Effective implementation requires clear land tenure arrangements, supportive regulations, and incentives for landowners and communities. Payment for ecosystem services programs, tax breaks, and subsidies can encourage participation, while community forestry initiatives empower local people to lead restoration efforts. Governance must also address potential trade-offs, ensuring that restoration does not displace communities, reduce food security, or prioritize commercial interests over ecological integrity.

Financing is another critical component of forest restoration strategies. Large-scale restoration requires significant investment, which can come from public budgets, international funds, or private sector engagement. Innovative financing mechanisms, such as green bonds, carbon markets, and blended finance, are increasingly used to support restoration projects. Aligning restoration with broader economic development goals can attract investment by demonstrating co-benefits such as job creation, water security, and disaster risk reduction. Partnerships between governments, businesses, NGOs, and communities are essential for mobilizing the financial and technical resources required.

Monitoring and adaptive management are fundamental to ensuring the success of restoration efforts. Restoration is a long-term process, and outcomes depend on factors that evolve over time. Remote sensing, geographic information systems, and ecological surveys provide tools to track progress, evaluate effectiveness, and adjust strategies as needed. Adaptive management recognizes that restoration must respond to uncertainties and changing conditions, making flexibility a key principle. Effective monitoring also contributes to transparency and accountability, building trust among stakeholders and demonstrating the value of restoration investments.

Forest restoration and reforestation strategies represent a convergence of ecological science, policy, and community action. They require integrating local knowledge with scientific expertise, aligning short-term incentives with long-term goals, and balancing ecological integrity with human development needs. Through natural regeneration, active reforestation, agroforestry, and landscape-level planning, forests can be restored to support biodiversity, climate stability, and human well-being. The growing momentum behind restoration reflects recognition that forests are indispensable for a sustainable future, and strategies for their recovery are central to global environmental and development agendas.

Grassland and Savanna Restoration

Grasslands and savannas cover vast regions of the Earth, supporting biodiversity, regulating climate, and providing livelihoods for millions of people. They are home to unique plant and animal communities, store large amounts of carbon in soils, and serve as vital grazing lands for livestock. Despite their importance, these ecosystems have often been undervalued and are frequently converted to croplands, degraded by overgrazing, or disrupted by invasive species and altered fire regimes. Restoration of grasslands and savannas is essential to safeguard their ecological integrity, enhance resilience to climate change, and sustain the communities that depend on them.

One of the primary challenges facing grasslands and savannas is overgrazing, which leads to soil compaction, erosion, and the loss of native vegetation. Restoration in such contexts often involves implementing sustainable grazing practices that balance livestock production with ecological health. Rotational grazing, resting degraded areas, and managing herd densities can allow vegetation to recover and soils to rebuild organic matter. In some cases, reducing livestock numbers or providing alternative fodder sources is necessary to relieve pressure on vulnerable areas. These approaches require collaboration with pastoral communities to ensure that restoration aligns with local livelihoods and cultural practices.

Fire plays a critical role in shaping grassland and savanna ecosystems. In many regions, fire is a natural disturbance that maintains ecological balance by preventing the encroachment of woody plants and promoting the regeneration of grasses. However, fire suppression policies or uncontrolled burning can disrupt this balance. Restoration strategies often focus on reintroducing controlled or prescribed burns that mimic natural fire regimes. Such interventions help maintain biodiversity, recycle nutrients, and sustain habitat for grazing animals. Careful planning and monitoring are essential to ensure that fire is used effectively and safely, taking into account ecological, social, and climatic conditions.

Invasive species pose another major threat to grassland and savanna ecosystems. Non-native plants often outcompete native grasses, reduce biodiversity, and alter ecological processes such as fire frequency and water availability. Restoration efforts may involve mechanical removal, targeted grazing, or the application of herbicides to control invasive species. Re-establishing native grasses and shrubs through reseeding or planting is also critical to ensure that ecosystems recover their original functions. These efforts require long-term commitment, as invasive species often return if management ceases prematurely.

Soil health restoration is central to grassland and savanna recovery. Degraded soils lose their capacity to retain water, cycle nutrients, and support vegetation. Techniques such as reseeding with deep-rooted native grasses, applying organic amendments, and using erosion-control measures like contour bunding can rebuild soil structure and fertility. Restoring vegetation cover is particularly important, as plant roots stabilize soils, enhance infiltration, and increase carbon storage. Healthy soils not only support biodiversity but also improve resilience to drought and climate variability.

Community involvement is critical for successful restoration of grasslands and savannas. Many of these landscapes are used for pastoralism, small-scale farming, or cultural practices. Restoration strategies that exclude local people are unlikely to succeed. Instead, participatory approaches that integrate traditional knowledge and provide tangible benefits to communities are more effective. For instance, involving pastoralists in fire management or providing incentives for sustainable grazing can encourage local stewardship. Restoration initiatives that create jobs, improve water availability, or enhance food security strengthen support and ensure long-term sustainability.

Grassland and savanna restoration also contributes to broader global goals. These ecosystems are significant carbon sinks, particularly through their soils, making their restoration an important climate mitigation strategy. Restoring grasslands improves water infiltration and storage, reducing flood risks and increasing water availability during dry periods. Biodiversity benefits include the return of pollinators, herbivores, and predators, which sustain ecological processes. By linking local restoration efforts to global priorities such as the Sustainable Development Goals and climate targets, these ecosystems gain greater recognition and resources for recovery.

Effective restoration requires integrating ecological science, local knowledge, and adaptive management. Each grassland and savanna system is unique, shaped by climate, soils, and human use, so strategies must be tailored to specific contexts. Monitoring is vital to assess progress and make adjustments, whether in grazing management, fire regimes, or invasive species control. Partnerships among governments, communities, NGOs, and researchers strengthen capacity and ensure that restoration is supported by both policy and practice.

Grassland and savanna restoration represents an opportunity to reconcile ecological sustainability with human development. By restoring vegetation, soils, and ecological processes, these ecosystems can once again provide the services that underpin life and livelihoods. The success of such efforts depends on balancing ecological integrity with social realities, ensuring that both nature and people benefit from the recovery of these vital landscapes.

Soil Restoration and Regenerative Practices

Soils are the foundation of terrestrial ecosystems and play a central role in supporting biodiversity, regulating water cycles, storing carbon, and providing the basis for food production. Healthy soils are living systems, teeming with microorganisms, fungi, and invertebrates that contribute to nutrient cycling, organic matter formation, and plant growth. Yet soils are increasingly under threat from intensive agriculture, deforestation, overgrazing, pollution, and urbanization. Degraded soils lose their fertility, structure, and capacity to retain water, making them highly vulnerable to erosion and desertification. Soil restoration and regenerative practices aim to reverse these trends by rebuilding soil health, enhancing ecological functions, and securing long-term productivity.

One of the central aspects of soil restoration is improving organic matter content. Organic matter, derived from decomposed plant and animal material, is critical for maintaining soil structure, fertility, and water-holding capacity. Practices such as compost application, cover cropping, and green manuring add organic material to soils, replenishing nutrients and supporting microbial activity. These techniques not only improve soil quality but also contribute to carbon sequestration, mitigating climate change. Restoring organic matter is often a long-term process, requiring sustained management to maintain inputs and avoid practices that deplete soil carbon.

Soil erosion is a major challenge in many landscapes, resulting from the removal of vegetation cover and unsustainable land use. Erosion strips away topsoil, the most fertile layer, and disrupts hydrological processes. Restoration strategies focus on stabilizing soils through re-vegetation, terracing, and contour farming. Planting native grasses and shrubs provides ground cover that protects soils from wind and water erosion, while root systems enhance soil cohesion. Structural measures such as check dams, bunds, and silt traps reduce runoff and capture sediments. These interventions, combined with sustainable land management, help rebuild soils and prevent further degradation.

Regenerative agriculture has emerged as a powerful framework for restoring soils while maintaining food production. Unlike conventional agriculture, which often relies on monocultures and heavy chemical inputs, regenerative practices focus on working with ecological processes. Crop diversification, minimal tillage, rotational grazing, and integration of livestock into cropping systems are central techniques. These approaches enhance soil biodiversity, improve nutrient cycling, and increase resilience to pests and climate variability. For example, reducing tillage minimizes soil disturbance, preserving structure and microbial communities, while rotational grazing allows pastures to recover and maintain ground cover. Regenerative agriculture demonstrates that soil restoration can align with productive farming, benefiting both ecosystems and farmers.

Water management is closely linked to soil restoration. Degraded soils often suffer from reduced infiltration and increased runoff, exacerbating water scarcity and erosion. Restoring soils involves practices that improve water retention and groundwater recharge. Techniques such as mulching, infiltration pits, and rainwater harvesting increase soil moisture availability, supporting vegetation growth and reducing drought vulnerability. In arid and semi-arid regions, zai pits, half-moons, and other traditional water-harvesting methods have proven effective in restoring degraded soils and boosting agricultural productivity. Linking soil restoration with water management ensures that both resources are conserved and enhanced.

Soil biodiversity is a key driver of ecosystem functions, yet it is often overlooked in restoration efforts. Microorganisms such as bacteria and fungi decompose organic matter, release nutrients, and build soil structure, while earthworms and other fauna aerate soils and enhance fertility. Restoring soil biodiversity requires reducing chemical inputs, avoiding practices that disrupt microbial communities, and reintroducing beneficial organisms where possible. Mycorrhizal inoculation, for instance, can enhance plant nutrient uptake and soil stability, while compost teas and biofertilizers stimulate microbial activity. By prioritizing soil life, restoration enhances resilience and productivity across ecosystems.

Policy and governance frameworks play an important role in scaling soil restoration. Land tenure security is essential for encouraging farmers and landholders to invest in long-term soil health. Incentives such as subsidies for regenerative practices, payment for ecosystem services, and carbon credits for soil carbon sequestration can motivate adoption. International initiatives, including the "4 per 1000" initiative launched under the Paris Agreement, emphasize the role of soils in mitigating climate change by increasing carbon stocks. Embedding soil restoration in agricultural, climate, and development policies ensures that efforts are supported by institutional structures and resources.

Community involvement is critical for the success of soil restoration programs. Farmers, pastoralists, and local communities are often the primary stewards of soils, and their knowledge and participation are indispensable. Traditional practices such as intercropping, composting, and agroforestry have long contributed to soil health and can be integrated with modern techniques. Training and extension services help build capacity, while participatory approaches ensure that restoration strategies reflect local needs and realities. Empowering communities fosters ownership, increasing the likelihood of sustained soil stewardship.

Monitoring and adaptive management are essential for effective soil restoration. Indicators such as soil organic carbon, infiltration rates, erosion levels, and microbial diversity provide insights into soil health and the effectiveness of interventions. Advances in technology, including remote sensing, digital mapping, and soil testing kits, enable more precise monitoring at multiple scales. Adaptive management allows practitioners to adjust practices in response to monitoring results, ensuring that restoration remains responsive to environmental and social conditions. Long-term monitoring is particularly important given the slow processes of soil recovery and the need to maintain improvements over time.

Soil restoration and regenerative practices are vital not only for ecological sustainability but also for food security, climate resilience, and human well-being. By rebuilding soil structure, fertility, and biodiversity, these practices create systems that are more productive, resilient, and sustainable. They demonstrate that human activity can shift from degrading soils to regenerating them, aligning agriculture and land use with ecological principles. Through a combination of organic amendments, erosion control, regenerative farming, water management, biodiversity enhancement, supportive policies, and community engagement, soils can be restored to sustain both nature and people for generations to come.

Combating Desertification and Land Degradation

Desertification and land degradation represent some of the most pressing environmental challenges of the modern era, affecting arid, semi-arid, and dry sub-humid regions around the world. These processes threaten the livelihoods of millions of people, reduce agricultural productivity, increase vulnerability to climate change, and contribute to biodiversity loss. Desertification is not the natural expansion of deserts but rather the degradation of land in drylands caused primarily by unsustainable human activities such as overgrazing, deforestation, poor irrigation practices, and inappropriate land use, compounded by climate variability. Combating desertification and land degradation requires comprehensive approaches that restore ecological functions, sustain livelihoods, and build resilience in vulnerable landscapes.

One of the central strategies in combating desertification is sustainable land management. This approach integrates ecological, economic, and social considerations to ensure that land use maintains productivity without compromising ecosystem health. Practices such as crop rotation, intercropping, and the use of drought-resistant varieties help maintain soil fertility and reduce pressure on fragile lands. Agroforestry systems, which combine trees and crops, are particularly effective in drylands, as they provide shade, reduce evaporation, enrich soils, and offer alternative income sources. By diversifying production and stabilizing ecosystems, sustainable land management reduces the drivers of degradation while supporting rural livelihoods.

Water management is another critical element in addressing desertification. Many degraded lands suffer from water scarcity, inefficient irrigation, and soil salinization. Techniques that enhance water availability and efficiency are essential for restoration. Traditional methods such as zai pits, terracing, and contour bunds capture rainfall and improve infiltration, while modern innovations like drip irrigation maximize water use efficiency. In regions where salinization is a problem, strategies include improving drainage, planting salt-tolerant species, and using soil amendments to restore fertility. By ensuring that water resources are used sustainably, these practices help prevent further land degradation and support vegetation recovery.

Revegetation and afforestation are widely used to restore degraded lands and stabilize drylands. Planting native grasses, shrubs, and trees can reduce wind and water erosion, improve soil structure, and create microclimates that support biodiversity. Shelterbelts and green barriers help protect farmland from desert winds and sand encroachment. Large-scale initiatives, such as the Great Green Wall in Africa, aim to restore millions of hectares of land through tree planting, agroforestry, and sustainable land practices. Successful revegetation depends on selecting appropriate species suited to local conditions and ensuring that communities are engaged in long-term stewardship.

Soil restoration is central to combating desertification. Degraded soils lose their capacity to retain nutrients and water, exacerbating land degradation. Practices such as adding organic matter, using compost, and integrating nitrogen-fixing plants improve soil fertility and structure. Conservation tillage minimizes soil disturbance, reducing erosion and maintaining soil cover. In drylands, techniques like mulching and cover cropping enhance soil moisture retention and reduce surface evaporation. Restoring soil health not only improves agricultural productivity but also strengthens resilience against droughts and climate shocks.

Community participation is vital for addressing desertification and land degradation. Local populations are often the most affected by these challenges, and their knowledge and involvement are critical for effective solutions. Participatory land-use planning, capacity-building programs, and incentives for sustainable practices ensure that restoration efforts align with local needs. Empowering women, who play a central role in managing natural resources in many regions, is particularly important. By involving communities, restoration projects gain social legitimacy and long-term sustainability.

Policy frameworks and international cooperation provide essential support for combating desertification. The United Nations Convention to Combat Desertification (UNCCD), established in 1994, is the leading international agreement focused on this issue. It promotes integrated strategies for sustainable land management, encourages financial and technical assistance, and fosters collaboration across nations. National action programs developed under the UNCCD guide countries in implementing strategies to prevent and reverse land degradation. Linking desertification efforts with broader climate and development agendas ensures that they receive the attention and resources required.

Monitoring and early warning systems play a crucial role in preventing desertification and managing degraded lands. Satellite imagery, remote sensing, and field-based assessments provide data on vegetation cover, soil conditions, and water availability. These tools allow governments and communities to detect early signs of degradation, evaluate the effectiveness of interventions, and adapt management strategies as needed. Building local capacity for monitoring ensures that responses are timely and context-specific.

Combating desertification and land degradation is not only an environmental priority but also a social and economic necessity. Healthy land supports food security, water availability, biodiversity, and climate resilience. By combining sustainable land management, effective water use, revegetation, soil restoration, community participation, and supportive policy frameworks, societies can halt and reverse degradation. These efforts create landscapes that are more productive, resilient, and capable of sustaining both people and ecosystems in the face of growing environmental challenges.

Chapter 3: Freshwater Ecosystem Restoration

Freshwater ecosystems—rivers, lakes, wetlands, and reservoirs—are vital lifelines that sustain biodiversity, regulate hydrological cycles, and provide clean water for agriculture, industry, and human consumption. Yet they are among the most degraded ecosystems on Earth, facing pressures from pollution, over-extraction, dam construction, invasive species, and climate change. Their decline threatens not only ecological health but also water security and resilience for communities worldwide. Restoring freshwater ecosystems is essential for rebuilding natural processes, safeguarding biodiversity, and ensuring reliable water resources for future generations. This chapter explores the principles, methods, and governance approaches guiding the restoration of freshwater systems.

River and Stream Restoration Approaches

Rivers and streams are dynamic ecosystems that provide freshwater, regulate landscapes, transport nutrients, and support biodiversity. They are central to human societies, supplying water for drinking, agriculture, industry, and energy production. Yet they are also among the most degraded ecosystems globally, impacted by dam construction, channelization, pollution, deforestation, and urban development. Restoration of rivers and streams seeks to re-establish ecological integrity, improve water quality, and restore natural processes that sustain both ecosystems and human needs. Effective approaches require a combination of ecological science, engineering, governance, and community engagement.

One of the most widely practiced strategies in river and stream restoration is re-naturalization of flow regimes. Alterations such as dams, diversions, and channel straightening disrupt hydrological processes, fragment habitats, and reduce ecological connectivity. Restoration often involves re-establishing more natural flow patterns by modifying dam operations, reconnecting floodplains, or removing obsolete structures. These actions help restore sediment transport, nutrient cycling, and fish migration. For example, dam removal projects in various regions have demonstrated how quickly rivers can recover, with improvements in water quality, habitat diversity, and species populations. Where full removal is not possible, flow releases or bypass channels can mimic natural variability and partially restore ecological functions.

Riparian zone restoration is another crucial approach. Vegetated areas along riverbanks stabilize soils, filter pollutants, provide shade, and support diverse species. Degraded riparian zones often result in erosion, sedimentation, and declining water quality. Restoration efforts typically involve replanting native vegetation, fencing to exclude livestock, and controlling invasive species. Restoring riparian buffers enhances habitat complexity, moderates water temperatures, and creates ecological corridors that connect terrestrial and aquatic ecosystems. In agricultural or urban landscapes, riparian restoration also provides co-benefits such as flood control and recreational opportunities.

Channel reconfiguration is often necessary in rivers and streams that have been straightened, incised, or armored with concrete. Natural channels typically have meanders, riffles, pools, and other features that support habitat diversity and ecological processes. Restoration techniques may involve re-meandering straightened sections, re-creating riffle-pool sequences, or adding woody debris and boulders to improve habitat complexity. These interventions slow water flow, reduce erosion, and increase habitat availability for fish, invertebrates, and plants. Engineered structures are sometimes used to guide channel adjustments, but success depends on designing interventions that mimic natural processes and adapt to changing hydrological conditions.

Water quality improvement is integral to river and stream restoration. Pollution from agriculture, industry, and urban runoff degrades aquatic ecosystems and reduces biodiversity. Restoration strategies focus on reducing pollutant inputs and enhancing natural purification processes. Constructed wetlands, buffer strips, and sediment traps can filter nutrients and contaminants before they reach rivers. Stream restoration also often involves reconnecting rivers with their floodplains, which act as natural filters by trapping sediments and assimilating nutrients. These approaches not only improve ecological health but also support human uses such as drinking water supply and recreation.

Habitat connectivity is critical for maintaining ecological integrity in river and stream systems. Many aquatic species rely on the ability to move freely along river corridors for feeding, breeding, and migration. Barriers such as dams, weirs, and culverts fragment habitats and block fish passage. Restoration approaches include installing fish ladders, bypass channels, or replacing barriers with more permeable structures. In some cases, removing barriers entirely is the most effective solution. Ensuring connectivity allows species populations to recover, genetic diversity to increase, and ecosystems to adapt more effectively to environmental changes.

Community and stakeholder engagement is an essential component of successful river and stream restoration. Rivers often flow through multiple jurisdictions and support diverse uses, including agriculture, energy, recreation, and cultural practices. Engaging communities in planning and implementation ensures that restoration efforts are socially acceptable, economically viable, and culturally relevant. Participatory approaches build trust, foster stewardship, and integrate local knowledge with scientific expertise. Restoration projects that provide visible benefits, such as improved fisheries, reduced flooding, or enhanced recreational opportunities, are more likely to gain long-term support and sustainability.

Monitoring and adaptive management underpin river and stream restoration approaches. Because rivers are dynamic and influenced by multiple factors, restoration outcomes are often uncertain and evolve over time. Monitoring physical, chemical, and biological indicators allows practitioners to assess progress, identify challenges, and adjust management strategies. Adaptive management emphasizes flexibility, recognizing that interventions must respond to new information and changing conditions such as climate variability. Long-term monitoring ensures that restoration goals are achieved and maintained across decades.

River and stream restoration represents a holistic approach to rebuilding ecosystems that sustain life and livelihoods. By re-establishing flow regimes, restoring riparian zones, reconfiguring channels, improving water quality, and enhancing connectivity, restoration efforts can repair ecological integrity and provide co-benefits for human societies. These approaches demonstrate that degraded rivers and streams are not lost causes but can be revitalized through coordinated efforts that blend ecological science, engineering, governance, and community participation.

Wetland Rehabilitation and Protection

Wetlands are among the most productive ecosystems on Earth, providing a wide range of ecological, social, and economic benefits. They regulate water flows, store and filter freshwater, support biodiversity, and act as significant carbon sinks. Wetlands also reduce flood risks by absorbing excess water, protect coastlines from storms, and provide livelihoods through fisheries, agriculture, and tourism. Despite their importance, wetlands are among the most threatened ecosystems, with more than half of the world's wetlands lost in the past century due to drainage, land conversion, pollution, and infrastructure development. Rehabilitation and protection of wetlands are therefore essential to sustain ecological integrity and human well-being.

Rehabilitation of wetlands begins with restoring their hydrology, as water is the defining feature of these ecosystems. Draining wetlands for agriculture or urban development disrupts natural water regimes, leading to soil degradation and biodiversity loss. Restoring hydrology often involves re-establishing natural water flows by removing drainage infrastructure, reconfiguring canals, or breaching levees. In cases where complete restoration of natural hydrology is not feasible, managed water releases or constructed inflows can simulate natural cycles. Hydrological restoration is fundamental because it revives ecological processes, supports wetland species, and reactivates the ecosystem's capacity to provide services such as water filtration and flood control.

Vegetation recovery is another key component of wetland rehabilitation. Native plants stabilize soils, improve water quality, and provide habitat for wildlife. Rehabilitation efforts often involve replanting or reseeding wetland vegetation, including reeds, sedges, and aquatic plants. Controlling invasive species is equally important, as they can outcompete native vegetation and alter ecosystem functions. Active management, such as mechanical removal or biological control, combined with promoting native vegetation, helps restore ecological balance. Healthy vegetation communities are vital for sustaining biodiversity and enhancing the resilience of wetlands to environmental changes.

Soil restoration plays a significant role in wetland recovery. Wetland soils, often rich in organic material, store large amounts of carbon and nutrients. When wetlands are drained, these soils degrade, releasing carbon dioxide and other greenhouse gases into the atmosphere. Rehabilitation strategies include re-wetting soils to prevent further emissions and promote the accumulation of organic matter. Re-establishing hydrology and vegetation cover also supports soil processes, improving fertility and stabilizing sediments. By restoring wetland soils, rehabilitation efforts contribute not only to ecosystem recovery but also to climate change mitigation through enhanced carbon sequestration.

Pollution control is critical for wetland rehabilitation and protection. Agricultural runoff, industrial discharges, and urban wastewater often introduce excessive nutrients, chemicals, and heavy metals into wetlands, degrading water quality and threatening biodiversity. Strategies to reduce pollution inputs include establishing buffer zones with vegetation, improving wastewater treatment, and promoting sustainable agricultural practices. In some cases, wetlands themselves are used as natural treatment systems, with constructed wetlands filtering contaminants before water enters natural ecosystems. Pollution control enhances the ecological health of wetlands and ensures that they continue to provide clean water and other services.

Protection of wetlands requires strong governance and policy frameworks. International agreements such as the Ramsar Convention on Wetlands, adopted in 1971, provide a global framework for conserving and sustainably using wetlands. Countries that are parties to the convention commit to designating wetlands of international importance and implementing policies for their wise use. National policies and regulations also play a crucial role in protecting wetlands from further degradation, while enforcement mechanisms ensure compliance. Integrating wetland protection into broader land-use planning and water management policies helps safeguard these ecosystems from competing demands.

Community involvement is essential for wetland rehabilitation and protection. Many wetlands are directly tied to local livelihoods, providing fish, fodder, building materials, and cultural values. Engaging communities in restoration projects ensures that local needs and knowledge are incorporated into management plans. Education and awareness programs help highlight the value of wetlands, building support for their protection. Involving local stakeholders fosters stewardship and increases the likelihood that rehabilitation efforts will be maintained in the long term. Successful wetland restoration often depends on aligning ecological goals with social and economic benefits for surrounding communities.

Monitoring and adaptive management strengthen wetland rehabilitation and protection. Wetlands are dynamic ecosystems, influenced by seasonal water cycles, climatic variability, and human activity. Continuous monitoring of water levels, vegetation, soil conditions, and biodiversity provides insights into the effectiveness of interventions. Adaptive management allows practitioners to respond to unexpected changes, refine strategies, and ensure that restoration objectives are met. Advances in remote sensing, GIS, and ecological modeling enhance monitoring capacity, enabling large-scale assessments of wetland health and progress toward restoration goals.

Wetland rehabilitation and protection are integral to addressing global challenges such as climate change, water scarcity, and biodiversity loss. By restoring hydrology, vegetation, and soils, reducing pollution, and strengthening governance, wetlands can regain their ecological functions and continue to support human societies. Protection through policies and community engagement ensures that restored wetlands are safeguarded for the future. These efforts highlight the unique role of wetlands as ecosystems that connect land and water, people and nature, and environmental sustainability with human development.

Lake and Reservoir Restoration

Lakes and reservoirs are vital freshwater ecosystems that provide drinking water, irrigation, fisheries, recreation, and habitat for diverse species. They also play a significant role in regulating hydrological and nutrient cycles. However, these systems are highly vulnerable to degradation from pollution, eutrophication, invasive species, sedimentation, and unsustainable water extraction. Reservoirs, while engineered, face many of the same challenges as natural lakes, and their ecological health is equally critical for sustaining the services they provide. Restoration of lakes and reservoirs focuses on reversing these impacts, improving water quality, restoring ecological functions, and ensuring sustainable use for both people and nature.

Eutrophication is one of the most widespread problems affecting lakes and reservoirs. Excessive inputs of nutrients, primarily nitrogen and phosphorus from agricultural runoff, sewage, and industrial effluents, stimulate algal blooms that reduce water quality, deplete oxygen, and harm aquatic life. Restoration strategies target both external and internal nutrient loads. Reducing external nutrient inputs involves improving agricultural practices, upgrading wastewater treatment, and establishing buffer zones of vegetation to intercept runoff. Addressing internal loads often requires techniques such as dredging nutrient-rich sediments, applying chemical treatments to bind phosphorus, or aerating water bodies to prevent anoxic conditions. By tackling nutrient enrichment, restoration efforts can significantly improve water quality and ecosystem health.

Hydrological management is another central aspect of lake and reservoir restoration. Over-extraction of water for irrigation, industry, or urban supply can lower water levels, disrupt ecological processes, and concentrate pollutants. In reservoirs, fluctuating water levels caused by dam operations can destabilize habitats and reduce biodiversity. Restoration efforts often involve adjusting water allocation to maintain ecological flows, improving reservoir operations to mimic natural hydrological cycles, and implementing integrated watershed management to balance competing demands. Ensuring adequate water availability supports aquatic ecosystems and enhances resilience to climate variability.

Sedimentation poses a significant challenge, especially in reservoirs where sediments accumulate over time, reducing storage capacity and water quality. Sediment originates from soil erosion in upstream catchments, often exacerbated by deforestation, agriculture, and poor land management. Restoration strategies include reducing sediment inflows through reforestation, soil conservation, and erosion-control measures in catchments. Within reservoirs, dredging or sediment flushing may be used to restore capacity, though these interventions are costly and disruptive. Long-term solutions emphasize watershed management, recognizing that healthy upstream landscapes are critical to sustaining downstream lakes and reservoirs.

Restoring biodiversity is a key objective of lake and reservoir rehabilitation. Degraded systems often experience declines in native species, proliferation of invasive species, and disruption of food webs. Restoration involves re-establishing habitat complexity through measures such as constructing artificial wetlands, reintroducing submerged vegetation, and installing structures like fish shelters. Controlling invasive species, whether aquatic plants such as water hyacinth or non-native fish, is also critical. Biodiversity restoration strengthens ecological processes, improves resilience, and enhances the cultural and recreational values of lakes and reservoirs.

Pollution control extends beyond nutrients to include industrial contaminants, heavy metals, plastics, and emerging pollutants such as pharmaceuticals. These substances accumulate in sediments and organisms, posing risks to ecosystems and human health. Restoration requires both regulatory and technical solutions, such as enforcing discharge limits, improving industrial practices, and implementing natural treatment systems. Constructed wetlands and riparian buffers can filter pollutants before they enter lakes, while sediment remediation techniques can address legacy pollution. A multi-pronged approach ensures that water quality improvements are sustained over the long term.

Community engagement and governance are essential for successful restoration. Lakes and reservoirs often serve multiple stakeholders with diverse and sometimes conflicting interests, from farmers and fishers to industries and urban populations. Inclusive governance frameworks that involve stakeholders in decision-making ensure that restoration strategies balance ecological and human needs. Community-based monitoring, education programs, and participatory management strengthen local stewardship and support compliance with restoration measures. Empowering communities fosters shared responsibility and enhances the sustainability of interventions.

Climate change adds new complexities to lake and reservoir restoration. Rising temperatures intensify thermal stratification, reduce dissolved oxygen, and increase the frequency of harmful algal blooms. Altered rainfall patterns affect water levels, inflows, and evaporation rates. Restoration strategies must therefore incorporate adaptive measures, such as selecting climate-resilient species for habitat restoration, designing flexible water management systems, and integrating climate scenarios into planning. Building resilience into restoration ensures that lakes and reservoirs can continue to function under changing conditions.

Monitoring and adaptive management are critical for evaluating progress and ensuring long-term success. Indicators such as nutrient concentrations, water clarity, oxygen levels, species diversity, and

41

sedimentation rates provide insights into ecological health. Advances in technology, including remote sensing, automated sensors, and modeling tools, enable continuous monitoring and predictive assessments. Adaptive management allows for adjustments in response to new challenges, ensuring that restoration efforts remain effective over time.

Restoration of lakes and reservoirs combines ecological science, engineering solutions, governance, and community participation. By addressing nutrient enrichment, managing water and sediment flows, restoring biodiversity, controlling pollution, and engaging stakeholders, these freshwater systems can recover their ecological integrity and continue to provide critical services. Rehabilitation efforts highlight the interdependence of catchments, water bodies, and human societies, underscoring the need for integrated approaches that sustain both ecosystems and people.

Watershed Management and Integrated Approaches

Watersheds are natural units that capture precipitation, channel water through rivers and streams, and deliver it to lakes, reservoirs, wetlands, and coastal areas. They integrate ecological, hydrological, and social systems across entire landscapes, making them a vital focus for environmental management. Healthy watersheds regulate water quality and quantity, recharge groundwater, support biodiversity, and provide essential resources for agriculture, industry, and households. However, pressures from deforestation, intensive agriculture, urbanization, pollution, and climate change have degraded many watersheds worldwide. Restoration and protection of watersheds require integrated approaches that combine ecological science, governance, and community engagement to address interlinked challenges at the basin scale.

At the heart of watershed management is the principle of integration. Water flows across boundaries of land use, jurisdictions, and sectors, meaning that interventions in one part of a watershed inevitably affect others. Integrated watershed management recognizes this interconnectedness, seeking to coordinate activities that influence water, soil, vegetation, and people. Rather than addressing single issues in isolation, such as pollution control or reforestation, integrated approaches consider the entire system, from headwaters to downstream areas. This ensures that restoration efforts enhance ecological processes while meeting the diverse needs of stakeholders.

Soil and land management play a critical role in watershed health. Erosion from agricultural fields, deforested slopes, or construction sites contributes to sedimentation in rivers, lakes, and reservoirs, reducing water quality and storage capacity. Integrated approaches prioritize soil conservation through practices such as terracing, contour plowing, agroforestry, and maintaining vegetation cover. By stabilizing soils, these measures reduce sediment flows, enhance infiltration, and improve agricultural productivity. Linking land restoration to water management helps ensure that upstream actions benefit downstream communities and ecosystems.

Water quality improvement is another essential focus. Pollutants from farms, industries, and urban runoff accumulate within watersheds, threatening both ecosystems and human health. Integrated approaches emphasize reducing pollution at the source through sustainable agricultural practices, better waste management, and green infrastructure in cities. Wetlands and riparian buffers are often restored or constructed to filter pollutants before they reach water bodies. By integrating land-use planning, wastewater treatment, and ecological restoration, watershed management can significantly enhance water quality while creating co-benefits such as habitat and recreation.

Flood and drought risk management also benefit from integrated watershed approaches. Restoring upstream forests, wetlands, and soils improves water retention and moderates runoff, reducing downstream flooding. Similarly, enhanced infiltration and groundwater recharge help buffer communities against drought. Structural measures, such as levees or reservoirs, are often complemented by ecological solutions, ensuring that natural processes work alongside engineering to build resilience. Managing risks at the watershed scale enables coordinated planning and reduces the vulnerability of both ecosystems and societies to climate variability and extreme events.

Governance is central to successful watershed management. Because watersheds often span multiple jurisdictions and involve competing interests, effective governance requires cooperation among governments, communities, businesses, and civil society. Multi-level governance frameworks create mechanisms for coordination, ensuring that policies and actions are aligned across local, regional, and national scales. Participatory approaches, including watershed councils and basin committees, give stakeholders a voice in decision-making, fostering trust and shared responsibility. Transparent governance and clear land and water rights are essential for balancing competing uses and sustaining restoration over the long term.

Financing integrated watershed management is a major challenge, given the scale and complexity of interventions. Blended finance mechanisms, including public funding, private investment, and international support, can provide resources for restoration. Payment for ecosystem services schemes offer incentives to upstream communities to manage land sustainably, benefiting downstream users with improved water supply and reduced risks. Linking watershed management to economic development—through improved agriculture, tourism, or energy generation—creates further justification for investment. Effective financial frameworks ensure that restoration is viable and that benefits are equitably shared among stakeholders.

Community participation is critical in watershed restoration. Local communities are often the primary managers of land and water, and their practices directly affect watershed health. Integrated approaches engage communities in planning, implementation, and monitoring, ensuring that interventions reflect local needs and knowledge. Empowering women and marginalized groups is especially important, as they are often disproportionately affected by resource degradation yet play crucial roles in managing natural resources. Building community ownership of watershed initiatives strengthens long-term sustainability and resilience.

Monitoring and adaptive management are essential for integrated watershed management. Because watersheds are dynamic and subject to changing social, ecological, and climatic conditions, restoration requires flexibility. Monitoring indicators such as water quality, flow regimes, soil health, and biodiversity provides insights into the effectiveness of interventions. Adaptive management allows strategies to be refined over time, ensuring that they remain responsive to emerging challenges. Advances in remote sensing, hydrological modeling, and digital monitoring tools provide powerful means for tracking changes at the watershed scale.

Watershed management and integrated approaches provide a comprehensive framework for addressing the complexity of land and water systems. By linking soil conservation, water quality, risk management, governance, financing, and community participation, these approaches restore ecological integrity while supporting human development. They highlight the importance of managing resources at the scale of natural systems, ensuring that restoration efforts are coordinated, inclusive, and resilient.

Chapter 4: Coastal and Marine Ecosystem Restoration

Coastal and marine ecosystems, including mangroves, seagrass meadows, coral reefs, and salt marshes, serve as critical buffers between land and sea while supporting immense biodiversity and providing livelihoods for millions of people. These ecosystems regulate climate, protect coastlines from storms, sustain fisheries, and store vast amounts of carbon. However, they are under severe threat from overfishing, pollution, coastal development, and the accelerating impacts of climate change, including ocean acidification and rising sea levels. Restoring coastal and marine ecosystems is fundamental to strengthening ecological resilience, safeguarding coastal communities, and sustaining global food and climate systems. This chapter examines strategies, technologies, and governance frameworks that drive effective restoration of marine environments.

Mangrove and Salt Marsh Restoration

Mangroves and salt marshes are critical coastal ecosystems that protect shorelines, support biodiversity, and provide essential ecosystem services. They act as natural barriers against storm surges, reduce coastal erosion, sequester significant amounts of carbon, and serve as nurseries for fish and other marine life. Despite their importance, both ecosystems have been extensively degraded or destroyed by land reclamation, aquaculture, agriculture, urban development, and pollution. Climate change, particularly sea level rise and increasing storm intensity, further threatens their survival. Restoration of mangroves and salt marshes has therefore become a global priority, recognized for its role in safeguarding coastal communities and advancing climate resilience.

Mangrove restoration often begins with re-establishing hydrological conditions. Mangroves thrive in intertidal zones where tidal flows regulate salinity, sediment deposition, and nutrient exchange. When hydrology is altered through dikes, roads, or other infrastructure, mangrove ecosystems decline. Effective restoration requires removing barriers or redesigning water flows to allow natural tidal exchange. Once hydrology is restored, natural regeneration is often possible, as mangroves readily recolonize when propagules are available. Where natural recovery is insufficient, planting mangrove seedlings may be necessary, though this must be carefully planned to match species with appropriate tidal and soil conditions.

Species selection is critical to successful mangrove restoration. Different mangrove species occupy specific ecological niches depending on salinity, inundation, and sediment characteristics. Planting inappropriate species or using monocultures can result in low survival rates and reduced ecosystem function. Restoring diverse assemblages of mangroves enhances resilience, biodiversity, and ecological integrity. Community nurseries and seed collection programs are often used to ensure a reliable supply of propagules, while local ecological knowledge helps identify suitable planting sites. Restoration that mimics natural zonation patterns is more likely to succeed in the long term.

Salt marsh restoration similarly emphasizes hydrological rehabilitation. Many salt marshes have been drained, diked, or converted for agriculture and development, disrupting tidal flows and altering salinity levels. Restoring natural hydrology by breaching levees, removing barriers, or creating channels allows tidal waters to re-enter and re-establish natural processes. Sediment management is also important, as salt marshes rely on sediment deposition to build elevation and keep pace with sea level rise. In some cases, thin-layer placement of dredged sediments is used to raise marsh surfaces, promoting vegetation growth and resilience.

Vegetation recovery in salt marshes involves reintroducing native plant species that stabilize soils and provide habitat for wildlife. Common species include cordgrasses and rushes, which tolerate saline and waterlogged conditions. Planting is often combined with measures to reduce grazing pressure and control invasive species such as common reed, which can displace native vegetation. Healthy plant communities trap sediments, enhance soil organic matter, and improve marsh resilience to storms and sea level rise. Vegetation also provides habitat for birds, fish, and invertebrates, reinforcing the ecological value of restored salt marshes.

The role of mangroves and salt marshes in carbon sequestration has attracted increasing attention. These ecosystems, often referred to as "blue carbon" systems, store carbon at rates far higher than terrestrial forests, particularly in their soils. Restoration therefore contributes not only to biodiversity and coastal protection but also to climate mitigation. Many countries are exploring the inclusion of mangrove and salt marsh restoration in their climate commitments under the Paris Agreement, and carbon finance mechanisms are being developed to support these efforts. By linking restoration to climate goals, financial and political support for coastal ecosystem recovery is expanding.

Community involvement is central to successful mangrove and salt marsh restoration. Coastal communities often depend on these ecosystems for livelihoods, including fishing, aquaculture, and tourism. Engaging communities in planning, planting, and monitoring ensures that restoration aligns with local needs and generates tangible benefits. Participatory approaches foster stewardship, build local capacity, and draw on traditional knowledge of coastal environments. In some regions, community-based restoration projects have become models of success, combining ecological recovery with improved income, food security, and disaster resilience.

Policy and governance frameworks provide the foundation for protecting and scaling restoration. National coastal management plans, integrated land-sea governance, and international agreements such as the Ramsar Convention support mangrove and salt marsh conservation. Legal protection of critical habitats, combined with enforcement mechanisms, prevents further loss. Economic incentives, such as payment for ecosystem services or support for sustainable aquaculture, create pathways for communities to balance restoration with livelihood needs. Cross-sectoral collaboration between governments, NGOs, businesses, and communities ensures that restoration is embedded within broader development and climate strategies.

Monitoring and adaptive management are essential in these dynamic coastal systems. Restoration outcomes depend on complex interactions among tides, sediments, vegetation, and climate, which evolve over time. Monitoring parameters such as vegetation cover, sediment accretion, hydrological conditions, and biodiversity provides data to evaluate progress and refine strategies. Adaptive management allows practitioners to respond to challenges such as storm damage, invasive species, or changing sea levels. Advances in remote sensing, drones, and ecological modeling enhance monitoring capacity, making large-scale assessments more feasible.

Mangrove and salt marsh restoration not only rehabilitates degraded ecosystems but also strengthens coastal resilience in the face of global environmental change. By re-establishing hydrology, restoring native vegetation, enhancing biodiversity, and engaging communities, these ecosystems can once again provide the protective and productive services on which millions of people rely. Their restoration represents a vital intersection of ecological recovery, climate action, and sustainable development, demonstrating how natural systems can be harnessed to safeguard both people and nature.

Seagrass and Coral Reef Restoration

Seagrass meadows and coral reefs are two of the most valuable marine ecosystems, providing habitat, food, and coastal protection while supporting fisheries and storing significant amounts of carbon. Despite their importance, both ecosystems have been severely degraded by human activities such as pollution, overfishing, coastal development, and destructive practices, as well as by the impacts of climate change. Their loss threatens marine biodiversity, local economies, and the resilience of coastal communities. Restoration of seagrasses and coral reefs has therefore become a central priority for global conservation efforts.

Seagrass restoration typically focuses on re-establishing meadows that have been damaged by dredging, nutrient pollution, or physical disturbance. One common approach is transplanting healthy seagrass shoots or sods from donor sites to degraded areas. In some cases, seagrass seeds are collected and directly sown into sediments to promote natural recolonization. These techniques require careful site selection, as seagrasses thrive in areas with suitable light levels, water quality, and sediment conditions. Restoring water quality is often a prerequisite, as seagrasses are highly sensitive to turbidity and excess nutrients. By improving conditions and reintroducing plants, seagrass restoration helps rebuild habitat complexity, enhance biodiversity, and stabilize sediments.

Seagrass ecosystems provide a wide range of benefits beyond habitat restoration. Their dense root systems anchor sediments, reducing erosion and improving water clarity. They also serve as nurseries for fish, shellfish, and other marine organisms, supporting local fisheries. Importantly, seagrasses are highly effective at storing carbon in their soils, contributing to climate mitigation efforts. Restoration of seagrass meadows therefore delivers multiple co-benefits, linking ecological recovery with economic and social gains. However, long-term success requires continuous monitoring and management to prevent renewed degradation from pollution or physical disturbance.

Coral reef restoration presents distinct challenges due to the complexity and sensitivity of reef ecosystems. One of the most widely used approaches is coral gardening, where fragments of healthy corals are grown in underwater nurseries before being transplanted to degraded reefs. These nurseries can be simple rope structures, frames, or more advanced floating systems that accelerate coral growth. Once mature, corals are outplanted onto reef structures, where they can establish and expand. Selecting resilient coral species, particularly those tolerant of warmer waters and bleaching, is increasingly emphasized to ensure restoration success under climate change.

Artificial reefs are another method used to restore coral ecosystems. Structures made from concrete, steel, or natural materials are deployed to provide surfaces for coral attachment and to create habitat for fish and invertebrates. These artificial reefs mimic the complexity of natural reefs, enhancing biodiversity and supporting fisheries. In some cases, 3D printing technology is used to design structures that replicate the intricate forms of natural corals, improving settlement and growth rates. While artificial reefs cannot fully replace natural ones, they provide valuable tools for enhancing degraded ecosystems.

Innovations in coral restoration also include techniques such as microfragmentation and assisted evolution. Microfragmentation involves breaking corals into tiny pieces, which then grow rapidly when reattached to substrates. Assisted evolution involves selectively breeding or conditioning corals to withstand stressors such as heat and acidification. These approaches aim to accelerate coral growth and increase resilience, addressing the urgent threats posed by climate change. Scaling up such innovations is critical to meet the pace of global reef decline.

Community engagement plays a pivotal role in seagrass and coral reef restoration. Coastal communities often depend directly on these ecosystems for food, income, and protection. Involving communities in planting, monitoring, and stewardship builds local ownership and ensures that restoration aligns with cultural and economic needs. Eco-tourism and sustainable fisheries can provide financial incentives for communities to protect restored ecosystems. Education and awareness programs further strengthen support, highlighting the long-term value of healthy seagrass meadows and coral reefs.

Policy frameworks and international initiatives provide crucial support for scaling restoration. Agreements such as the Convention on Biological Diversity and the Paris Agreement emphasize the role of blue carbon ecosystems, including seagrasses and coral reefs, in achieving global biodiversity and climate goals. Regional frameworks, such as marine protected areas, safeguard critical habitats while supporting restoration efforts. Financial mechanisms, including carbon credits and payment for ecosystem services, are emerging as tools to incentivize investment in marine restoration. Embedding these ecosystems into global agendas strengthens political and financial backing for large-scale recovery.

Monitoring and adaptive management are essential to ensure the long-term success of restoration projects. For seagrasses, monitoring involves tracking shoot density, water quality, sediment stability, and biodiversity. For coral reefs, indicators include coral cover, species diversity, recruitment rates, and bleaching resistance. Adaptive management enables practitioners to respond to new challenges, such as climate shocks, disease outbreaks, or invasive species. Advances in technology, including drones, satellite imagery, and underwater robotics, enhance monitoring capacity and enable larger-scale assessments.

Restoring seagrass meadows and coral reefs is both a scientific and societal challenge, requiring ecological knowledge, innovative techniques, supportive policies, and community engagement. By rebuilding these ecosystems, restoration efforts protect biodiversity, sustain livelihoods, and strengthen resilience to climate change. Their recovery demonstrates the potential of marine restoration not only to heal damaged ecosystems but also to secure a sustainable future for coastal communities and the planet.

Addressing Marine Pollution and Habitat Degradation

Marine ecosystems are increasingly threatened by pollution and habitat degradation, undermining their capacity to sustain biodiversity, support fisheries, regulate climate, and provide livelihoods for millions of people. Pollution enters oceans and coastal waters through multiple pathways, including agricultural runoff, industrial discharges, untreated sewage, oil spills, and plastics. Habitat degradation results from destructive practices such as bottom trawling, coastal development, sand mining, and unregulated tourism. Together, these pressures diminish water quality, disrupt food webs, and weaken the resilience of marine ecosystems to climate change. Addressing marine pollution and habitat degradation requires coordinated actions that integrate science, governance, and community engagement to safeguard ocean health.

Nutrient pollution is one of the most significant challenges. Excess nitrogen and phosphorus from fertilizers, livestock waste, and sewage promote harmful algal blooms, which reduce oxygen levels, block sunlight, and create dead zones where marine life cannot survive. Addressing nutrient pollution involves improving agricultural practices, such as precision fertilization, buffer strips, and constructed wetlands to filter runoff. Upgrading wastewater treatment facilities and reducing sewage discharge into coastal waters are equally critical. Restoring wetlands and mangroves also enhances natural nutrient filtering, linking pollution control with habitat restoration.

Plastic pollution has become a defining environmental issue of the 21st century. Each year, millions of tons of plastic enter oceans, where they entangle wildlife, are ingested by marine organisms, and break down into microplastics that accumulate in food chains. Strategies to address plastic pollution include reducing single-use plastics, improving recycling systems, and promoting circular economy models that design products for reuse. Cleanup initiatives, from coastal cleanups to large-scale ocean plastic collection systems, also play a role, though prevention remains the most effective solution. Policies such as bans on certain plastics, extended producer responsibility, and incentives for sustainable packaging support systemic change to reduce plastic flows into the ocean.

Chemical and industrial pollution also pose serious risks to marine ecosystems. Heavy metals, oil, pesticides, and other contaminants accumulate in sediments and organisms, threatening biodiversity and human health. Addressing these pollutants requires stricter regulations on industrial discharges, improved monitoring, and enforcement of international agreements such as the International Convention for the Prevention of Pollution from Ships (MARPOL).

In cases of legacy pollution, remediation strategies such as sediment dredging, capping, or bioremediation may be necessary. Strengthening governance frameworks ensures accountability and reduces the risks of chronic contamination.

Habitat degradation is closely linked to marine pollution, often amplifying its effects. Destructive fishing practices such as bottom trawling physically damage seafloor habitats, including coral reefs and seagrass meadows. Coastal development and sand mining alter natural hydrology and erode habitats, while unregulated tourism can degrade fragile ecosystems through anchor damage, trampling, and pollution. Addressing these pressures involves promoting sustainable fisheries management, establishing marine protected areas, and enforcing regulations that limit destructive activities. Integrating habitat considerations into coastal planning ensures that development balances economic benefits with ecological protection.

Marine protected areas (MPAs) are one of the most effective tools for addressing habitat degradation. By restricting harmful activities and allowing ecosystems to recover, MPAs safeguard biodiversity and restore ecological functions. Effective MPAs are not only well-designed and ecologically representative but also supported by strong governance and enforcement. Linking MPAs with broader marine spatial planning ensures that conservation is balanced with sustainable use. Expanding networks of MPAs contributes to global biodiversity goals while enhancing resilience to pollution and climate change.

Community engagement and local stewardship are central to tackling marine pollution and habitat degradation. Coastal communities often bear the brunt of ecosystem decline, experiencing reduced fisheries, declining tourism, and increased vulnerability to storms. Involving communities in monitoring, restoration, and sustainable resource management strengthens ownership and ensures that interventions align with local priorities. Initiatives such as community-based fisheries management, eco-tourism, and citizen science projects empower people to become active stewards of marine environments.

Education and awareness programs further build support for reducing pollution and protecting habitats.

International cooperation is critical given the transboundary nature of marine pollution. Plastics, oil, and chemicals travel across borders through ocean currents, while atmospheric deposition spreads pollutants globally. Agreements such as the United Nations Convention on the Law of the Sea (UNCLOS) and the Global Programme of Action for the Protection of the Marine Environment from Land-based Activities provide frameworks for coordinated action. Regional initiatives, such as the Regional Seas Programmes, bring neighboring countries together to address shared challenges. Strengthening these cooperative frameworks ensures that marine pollution is managed at the scales necessary for effectiveness.

Monitoring and adaptive management are essential for addressing pollution and habitat degradation. Advances in technology, such as satellite imagery, autonomous underwater vehicles, and environmental DNA, enable better detection of pollutants and assessment of ecosystem health. Monitoring provides data to evaluate interventions, enforce regulations, and adapt strategies to changing conditions. Building capacity for monitoring in developing countries is particularly important, as many of the most affected regions have limited resources to address these challenges.

Addressing marine pollution and habitat degradation requires systemic change, integrating prevention, remediation, and protection. By reducing nutrient and plastic inputs, controlling chemical pollutants, restoring habitats, enforcing sustainable practices, and engaging communities, societies can begin to reverse the decline of marine ecosystems. These actions not only protect biodiversity but also secure the essential services that oceans provide, from food and livelihoods to climate regulation and coastal defense.

Sustainable Fisheries and Marine Biodiversity Recovery

Fisheries are vital to global food security, livelihoods, and cultures, providing protein for billions of people and employment for millions worldwide. However, decades of overfishing, illegal and unregulated practices, destructive gear use, and weak governance have pushed many fish stocks beyond sustainable levels. Alongside these pressures, marine biodiversity faces unprecedented threats from habitat loss, pollution, climate change, and ocean acidification. Restoring marine biodiversity and ensuring sustainable fisheries are therefore deeply interconnected goals, requiring coordinated strategies that balance ecological health with human needs.

Central to sustainable fisheries is the principle of maintaining fish populations at levels that allow for long-term productivity. Overfishing reduces reproductive capacity, disrupts food webs, and destabilizes ecosystems. Implementing science-based management, such as setting catch limits, size restrictions, and seasonal closures, is essential to allow stocks to recover. Ecosystem-based fisheries management (EBFM) goes further by considering the broader ecological context, including predator-prey relationships, habitat requirements, and environmental variability. This approach recognizes that fisheries cannot be managed in isolation but must account for the health of entire marine ecosystems.

Marine biodiversity recovery requires protecting critical habitats that sustain fish populations and other marine life. Coral reefs, seagrass meadows, mangroves, and estuaries serve as nurseries and feeding grounds for countless species. Restoring these habitats directly benefits fisheries by supporting recruitment and maintaining ecological processes. Sustainable fisheries and habitat conservation thus reinforce one another, creating synergies that enhance both food security and biodiversity. Effective protection of spawning grounds, migration routes, and nursery areas is particularly important for rebuilding depleted populations.

Addressing illegal, unreported, and unregulated (IUU) fishing is a major challenge for marine biodiversity recovery. IUU fishing undermines management systems, threatens livelihoods, and accelerates resource depletion. Strengthening monitoring, control, and surveillance systems is vital, using tools such as vessel monitoring systems, satellite tracking, and international enforcement agreements. Transparency in supply chains, including certification and traceability, helps ensure that seafood comes from legal and sustainable sources. International cooperation is essential, as fish stocks often cross national boundaries and high seas governance requires collective action.

Gear technology and fishing practices also play a crucial role in sustainability. Destructive practices such as bottom trawling damage habitats and cause high levels of bycatch, harming non-target species including turtles, dolphins, and seabirds. Transitioning to selective gear that reduces bycatch and minimizes habitat damage is a key strategy. Innovations such as turtle excluder devices, circle hooks, and modified nets have proven effective in reducing ecological impacts. Promoting low-impact fishing methods ensures that fisheries can operate while maintaining marine biodiversity.

Marine protected areas (MPAs) are one of the most powerful tools for supporting both fisheries recovery and biodiversity conservation. By restricting or prohibiting extractive activities in designated zones, MPAs allow ecosystems to recover and replenish adjacent fishing grounds through spillover effects. Well-designed and effectively managed MPAs safeguard biodiversity hotspots, restore ecological balance, and contribute to sustainable fisheries. Expanding global MPA networks, alongside other area-based measures such as seasonal closures and gear restrictions, strengthens resilience across marine ecosystems.

Climate change poses additional challenges to sustainable fisheries and biodiversity recovery. Warming waters, ocean acidification, and shifting species distributions alter the productivity and composition of marine ecosystems. Adaptation strategies include developing flexible management systems that can respond to changing stock distributions, protecting climate refugia, and diversifying livelihoods in coastal communities. Restoring biodiversity enhances resilience, as ecosystems with greater diversity are better able to absorb and adapt to environmental change. Integrating climate considerations into fisheries and conservation policies ensures long-term sustainability.

Community-based management is a cornerstone of sustainable fisheries and biodiversity recovery. Coastal communities often depend directly on marine resources and possess detailed knowledge of local ecosystems. Engaging communities in decision-making fosters stewardship, compliance, and adaptive management. Examples include locally managed marine areas (LMMAs), which empower communities to set rules for resource use and enforce them. Linking conservation outcomes with livelihood benefits— through eco-tourism, value-added seafood products, or payments for ecosystem services—creates incentives for sustainable practices and biodiversity protection.

Economic and policy instruments further support sustainable fisheries. Certification schemes such as the Marine Stewardship Council (MSC) create market incentives for sustainable practices, rewarding fisheries that meet environmental and social standards. Subsidy reform is also critical, as harmful subsidies often encourage overfishing and excess capacity. Redirecting financial support toward sustainable practices, research, and monitoring strengthens governance and promotes recovery. International frameworks, including the United Nations Sustainable Development Goals and the Convention on Biological Diversity, provide global commitments that guide national action on fisheries and biodiversity.

Monitoring and scientific research underpin all efforts to restore marine biodiversity and sustain fisheries. Data on stock levels, ecosystem health, and fishing effort are essential for adaptive management. Emerging technologies, including environmental DNA (eDNA), satellite monitoring, and artificial intelligence, are expanding capacity to assess ecosystems and enforce regulations. Continuous evaluation ensures that policies remain effective, equitable, and responsive to ecological and social changes. Building scientific capacity, particularly in developing regions, is critical to ensure global progress.

Sustainable fisheries and marine biodiversity recovery represent intertwined goals that require integrated approaches across ecological, economic, and social dimensions. By combining science-based management, habitat restoration, enforcement against illegal practices, technological innovation, community stewardship, and supportive policies, societies can restore ocean health while maintaining vital food and livelihood systems. These efforts not only rebuild fish stocks and biodiversity but also strengthen resilience, ensuring that marine ecosystems can continue to sustain future generations.

Chapter 5: Urban Ecosystem Restoration

Urban ecosystems are increasingly central to global sustainability, as more than half of the world's population now lives in cities. Rapid urbanization has often come at the expense of natural systems, resulting in the loss of green spaces, the degradation of rivers and wetlands, and heightened vulnerability to climate risks such as flooding, heatwaves, and poor air quality. Restoring ecosystems within cities is not only about bringing nature back into urban landscapes but also about improving public health, enhancing resilience, and creating more livable environments. This chapter explores the principles, tools, and strategies for restoring urban ecosystems, highlighting their role in shaping sustainable and inclusive cities of the future.

Green Infrastructure and Urban Greening

Green infrastructure and urban greening are increasingly recognized as essential strategies for enhancing the resilience, sustainability, and livability of cities. As urban populations grow and climate pressures intensify, cities face challenges such as heat stress, flooding, air pollution, and biodiversity loss. Traditional infrastructure systems, dominated by concrete and steel, often exacerbate these issues by sealing soils, channeling stormwater rapidly into drainage systems, and providing little habitat for nature. Green infrastructure provides a complementary and sometimes alternative approach, using natural and semi-natural systems to deliver ecological, social, and economic benefits within urban areas.

Green infrastructure refers to strategically planned networks of natural and constructed green spaces that provide ecosystem services and connect people with nature. It includes features such as parks, urban forests, green roofs, rain gardens, bioswales, and restored rivers. By integrating vegetation and ecological functions into the fabric of cities, green infrastructure supports climate adaptation, enhances biodiversity, and improves quality of life. Urban greening, a closely related concept, emphasizes the widespread introduction of vegetation into urban areas, from street trees to community gardens, with the goal of creating healthier and more attractive environments.

One of the primary functions of green infrastructure is managing stormwater. Conventional drainage systems channel water quickly into sewers, often leading to flooding during heavy rains and polluting waterways with untreated runoff. Green infrastructure slows, absorbs, and filters stormwater through natural processes, reducing peak flows and improving water quality. Green roofs capture rainfall, bioswales direct and filter runoff along streets, and rain gardens infiltrate water into soils. These systems mimic natural hydrology, reduce pressure on drainage networks, and increase urban resilience to climate extremes.

Urban greening also plays a critical role in mitigating the urban heat island effect. Cities often experience higher temperatures than surrounding rural areas due to heat-absorbing materials such as asphalt and concrete, limited vegetation, and concentrated human activity. Planting trees, creating green walls, and expanding parks help cool cities through shading and evapotranspiration. Cooler urban environments improve public health by reducing heat-related illnesses and energy demand for air conditioning. Greener streetscapes also make cities more comfortable and attractive, encouraging walking and cycling as sustainable modes of transport.

Biodiversity conservation is another benefit of green infrastructure and urban greening. Urbanization fragments and reduces habitats, threatening many species. By creating interconnected green spaces, cities can provide habitat for birds, insects, and other wildlife, supporting urban biodiversity. Urban forests, wetlands, and pocket parks contribute to ecological connectivity, enabling species movement and genetic exchange. Community initiatives such as pollinator gardens and native plantings further enhance biodiversity while fostering environmental stewardship among residents.

Social and cultural benefits are central to urban greening. Access to green spaces improves mental health, reduces stress, and promotes physical activity. Parks and community gardens foster social cohesion by providing spaces for recreation, cultural expression, and community events. Urban greening initiatives can also address equity issues by targeting investments in underserved neighborhoods that historically lack access to quality green spaces. By integrating cultural values and community needs into design, green infrastructure projects can strengthen social resilience alongside ecological resilience.

Economic benefits complement the ecological and social gains. Green infrastructure can reduce infrastructure costs by lowering flood damage, cooling cities, and extending the lifespan of gray infrastructure through complementary functions. It also increases property values, attracts investment, and supports tourism. Job creation in sectors such as landscape management, ecological restoration, and green technology further reinforces its economic value. By aligning environmental objectives with financial benefits, green infrastructure presents a cost-effective approach to sustainable urban development.

Effective implementation of green infrastructure and urban greening requires strong governance and planning. Policies and regulations that integrate ecological design into zoning, building codes, and urban planning frameworks are essential. Multi-sector collaboration between governments, businesses, NGOs, and communities ensures that projects are well-resourced and inclusive. Financing mechanisms such as green bonds, public-private partnerships, and payment for ecosystem services can provide sustainable funding. Monitoring and evaluation frameworks help measure outcomes, refine strategies, and demonstrate the value of green investments to decision-makers.

Urban greening is increasingly being linked with climate adaptation and mitigation strategies. By reducing heat, managing floods, storing carbon, and providing renewable resources, green infrastructure contributes to both adaptation and emission reduction goals. Cities around the world are embedding green infrastructure into climate action plans, recognizing its role in building resilience and sustainability. Global initiatives and networks further support knowledge exchange and scaling, enabling cities to learn from each other's experiences.

Green infrastructure and urban greening represent a transformative shift in how cities are designed and managed. They demonstrate that ecological systems can function alongside built infrastructure to address pressing urban challenges. By integrating vegetation, water management, biodiversity, and community engagement into the heart of urban planning, cities can create environments that are healthier, more resilient, and more equitable. These approaches highlight the potential of nature-based solutions to secure sustainable urban futures in the face of global environmental change.

Restoring Urban Rivers and Wetlands

Urban rivers and wetlands play a crucial role in maintaining ecological balance, supporting biodiversity, and enhancing the livability of cities. Historically, many of these systems have been heavily modified to accommodate urban growth, with rivers channelized or diverted and wetlands drained for development. These interventions have reduced water quality, increased flood risks, and degraded habitats. Restoring urban rivers and wetlands seeks to reverse these impacts by re-establishing natural processes, improving ecological functions, and creating multifunctional landscapes that benefit both people and nature.

One of the primary goals of urban river restoration is re-naturalizing channels that have been engineered for flood control or navigation. Many urban rivers were straightened, lined with concrete, or placed in culverts, reducing their ability to support biodiversity and regulate water flows. Restoration approaches include removing hard infrastructure, reintroducing meanders, and reconnecting rivers with their floodplains. These measures slow water flow, enhance sediment deposition, and create diverse habitats. In addition to ecological benefits, re-naturalized rivers provide recreational opportunities, improve aesthetics, and strengthen urban resilience to climate change.

Wetland restoration in urban areas similarly focuses on re-establishing hydrological and ecological functions. Wetlands act as natural water filters, removing pollutants and excess nutrients from runoff, while also storing floodwaters and recharging groundwater. Restoring urban wetlands often involves removing fill, re-wetting soils, and planting native vegetation. Constructed wetlands can also be created in highly modified landscapes, designed to mimic natural systems while providing stormwater management and habitat functions. These wetlands support birdlife, amphibians, and aquatic species, contributing to urban biodiversity while improving water quality.

Water quality improvement is a central outcome of restoring urban rivers and wetlands. Urban runoff typically carries pollutants such as heavy metals, hydrocarbons, and nutrients into waterways, degrading ecological health. Restored rivers and wetlands act as natural treatment systems, trapping sediments, filtering contaminants, and assimilating nutrients. Vegetated buffers along waterways further enhance filtration and reduce pollutant loads. By improving water quality, restoration not only benefits ecosystems but also safeguards human health and expands opportunities for recreation and education.

Restoration projects increasingly integrate green infrastructure to manage stormwater and reduce flooding. Bioswales, rain gardens, and permeable pavements can divert and filter runoff before it reaches rivers and wetlands, reducing peak flows and pollution. Integrating these measures into urban landscapes complements restoration efforts by reducing pressure on natural systems. Linking urban planning with ecological design ensures that rivers and wetlands function as part of broader networks that deliver multiple ecosystem services.

Community engagement is vital for successful restoration in urban contexts. Rivers and wetlands often intersect with neighborhoods, industries, and cultural spaces, creating diverse interests and values. Engaging communities in planning, design, and stewardship fosters local ownership and ensures that restoration reflects social priorities. Public spaces created through restoration projects provide opportunities for recreation, cultural expression, and education, helping to reconnect urban residents with natural systems. Volunteer programs, citizen science initiatives, and school projects also strengthen community ties to restored environments.

Governance and policy frameworks provide the institutional support needed for restoration. Integrating river and wetland restoration into urban development plans ensures that ecological priorities are considered alongside housing, transport, and economic growth. Policies that protect riparian zones, incentivize green infrastructure, and enforce water quality standards create enabling conditions for restoration. Partnerships among governments, NGOs, businesses, and communities mobilize resources and expertise, making large-scale interventions possible. Aligning restoration with broader climate adaptation and sustainability agendas further strengthens political and financial support.

Monitoring and adaptive management ensure the long-term success of restoration projects. Urban environments are dynamic, with pressures from population growth, pollution, and climate variability. Continuous monitoring of water quality, biodiversity, and hydrological conditions provides insights into the effectiveness of interventions. Adaptive management allows for adjustments as conditions change, ensuring that restoration objectives remain achievable. Advances in technologies such as remote sensing, drones, and environmental DNA enhance monitoring capacity, providing detailed data for decision-making.

Restoring urban rivers and wetlands is more than an ecological necessity; it is a pathway to creating healthier, more resilient, and more sustainable cities. By re-naturalizing waterways, rehabilitating wetlands, improving water quality, and integrating community priorities, these projects deliver multiple benefits. They reduce flood risks, enhance biodiversity, provide green spaces, and improve urban well-being. In the face of accelerating urbanization and climate change, restoring rivers and wetlands demonstrates how cities can reconnect with nature to build sustainable futures.

Enhancing Biodiversity in Cities

Biodiversity in urban areas is often overlooked, yet cities can host a wide array of species and play an important role in conservation. As urbanization expands, natural habitats are fragmented or lost, and many species are displaced. However, cities also present opportunities to create new habitats, restore ecological functions, and reconnect people with nature. Enhancing biodiversity in cities involves integrating ecological principles into planning, design, and management, ensuring that urban environments support both wildlife and human well-being.

Urban green spaces are central to supporting biodiversity. Parks, gardens, green roofs, and urban forests provide habitats for birds, insects, and small mammals. Designing these spaces with native plants enhances ecological value, as native species are better adapted to local conditions and provide food and shelter for wildlife. Connectivity between green spaces is equally important, as fragmented habitats limit the movement of species. Green corridors, riparian buffers, and tree-lined streets create pathways that allow organisms to move across the city, maintaining genetic diversity and resilience.

Water bodies also contribute to urban biodiversity. Restored rivers, ponds, and wetlands provide habitats for fish, amphibians, and aquatic invertebrates while supporting migratory birds. Incorporating naturalized edges and vegetation enhances ecological complexity, offering shelter and breeding grounds. Stormwater management systems designed as constructed wetlands or bioswales can serve dual purposes, reducing flooding risks and supporting biodiversity.

These blue-green infrastructures demonstrate how ecological functions can be integrated into essential urban systems.

Urban biodiversity is not only about quantity but also about quality. Diverse habitats support more complex ecological communities, strengthening resilience to pests, diseases, and climate variability. Introducing vertical greening, rooftop gardens, and pocket parks in densely built environments expands habitat opportunities where space is limited. Even small-scale interventions, such as pollinator gardens or native hedgerows, can significantly enhance ecological networks. These measures contribute to the survival of urban-adapted species and create stepping stones that connect larger green areas.

Community engagement is vital for enhancing biodiversity in cities. Urban residents influence local ecosystems through gardening choices, land management, and recreational activities. Programs that encourage residents to plant native species, create wildlife-friendly gardens, or participate in citizen science projects increase awareness and participation in biodiversity efforts. Schools, universities, and community groups play key roles in promoting environmental education and stewardship. By involving people directly, biodiversity initiatives foster a sense of ownership and ensure long-term sustainability.

Governance and policy frameworks provide the foundation for urban biodiversity. Integrating biodiversity targets into land-use planning, zoning regulations, and infrastructure development ensures that ecological considerations are not sidelined. Urban biodiversity strategies often align with broader goals, such as climate adaptation, health, and sustainable development. For example, policies supporting tree planting contribute to biodiversity while also mitigating heat islands, improving air quality, and enhancing public spaces. Cross-sector collaboration among governments, NGOs, and private actors strengthens resources and ensures that biodiversity is embedded into urban growth.

Economic incentives further support urban biodiversity. Green infrastructure projects that enhance biodiversity often reduce costs associated with stormwater management, air pollution, and heat mitigation. Property values tend to increase in areas with rich green spaces, encouraging investment in biodiversity-friendly designs. Eco-tourism and recreational opportunities also generate economic benefits, highlighting the links between biodiversity and urban prosperity. Financing mechanisms such as green bonds or payment for ecosystem services can provide long-term support for biodiversity initiatives.

Monitoring and adaptive management are essential for maintaining biodiversity gains in cities. Tracking species diversity, habitat quality, and ecological connectivity provides insights into the effectiveness of interventions. Advances in technology, including remote sensing, environmental DNA, and smartphone applications, make monitoring more accessible and inclusive. Adaptive management ensures that strategies can be refined in response to ecological or social changes, keeping biodiversity initiatives relevant and effective.

Enhancing biodiversity in cities transforms urban environments into spaces that are not only functional but also ecologically rich and socially vibrant. By integrating green infrastructure, restoring habitats, engaging communities, and embedding biodiversity into governance and policy, cities can support diverse species while improving the health and well-being of residents. Biodiversity-rich cities demonstrate that urban development and nature need not be in conflict but can coexist in ways that create sustainable and resilient futures.

Ecosystem Services in Urban Planning

Ecosystem services are the benefits that humans derive from nature, including clean air and water, climate regulation, food production, and cultural values. In urban contexts, ecosystem services are particularly important because cities concentrate people, infrastructure, and economic activity in areas that often experience environmental stress. Integrating ecosystem services into urban planning provides a framework for designing cities that are not only functional but also sustainable, resilient, and supportive of human well-being.

Urban ecosystems, including parks, rivers, wetlands, forests, and green roofs, supply a wide range of services that address pressing urban challenges. Regulating services such as stormwater management, temperature moderation, and air purification directly improve urban living conditions. For example, trees absorb pollutants, cool neighborhoods through shading, and reduce energy demand for cooling. Wetlands and rivers act as natural water filters and buffers against floods, reducing infrastructure costs while protecting communities. By recognizing these functions as services, urban planning can integrate ecological processes into design and management.

Provisioning services are equally relevant in cities, even though urban environments are not primary sites of food or raw material production. Community gardens, urban agriculture, and rooftop farms provide fresh food, contribute to food security, and reduce dependence on distant supply chains. Urban forests and green belts can also provide timber, fuelwood, and non-timber forest products. While these provisioning services may be smaller in scale compared to rural areas, their contributions to resilience and local economies are significant.

Cultural services are among the most visible in urban environments. Access to green spaces improves mental and physical health, offering opportunities for recreation, relaxation, and social interaction. Parks, riversides, and nature trails foster community cohesion and enhance the aesthetic and cultural value of cities. Cultural ecosystem services also include educational opportunities, such as nature-based learning in schools and environmental awareness programs. These intangible benefits play a vital role in enhancing quality of life and building support for conservation in cities.

Supporting services underpin the long-term functioning of urban ecosystems. Processes such as soil formation, nutrient cycling, and pollination are often overlooked but are critical to sustaining life in cities. Pollinators support urban agriculture, while healthy soils ensure that vegetation can thrive and provide other ecosystem services. By incorporating these processes into urban planning, cities can strengthen ecological resilience and avoid costly interventions to replace degraded functions.

Integrating ecosystem services into urban planning requires a shift in perspective. Traditional planning often prioritizes built infrastructure and economic development, viewing nature as a constraint or afterthought. A services-based approach reframes ecosystems as assets that deliver essential functions and should be actively managed. Tools such as ecosystem service mapping, valuation, and accounting help planners identify the spatial distribution of services and assess their contributions to urban systems. These tools also support decision-making by highlighting trade-offs between development and conservation.

Policy frameworks are essential for embedding ecosystem services into planning. Land-use regulations, zoning policies, and environmental standards can be designed to protect and enhance ecological assets. Incentives such as tax breaks, green building certifications, and subsidies for green infrastructure encourage investment in ecosystem services. At the international level, frameworks such as the Sustainable Development Goals and the Convention on Biological Diversity promote the integration of ecosystem services into urban policy. Aligning local planning with these global goals strengthens the case for ecological approaches.

Governance plays a critical role in operationalizing ecosystem services in cities. Urban ecosystems often span multiple jurisdictions and involve diverse stakeholders, from government agencies to communities and businesses. Collaborative governance structures ensure that services are managed collectively and equitably. Participation by local communities enhances legitimacy, builds trust, and ensures that interventions reflect local needs and knowledge.

Effective governance also includes monitoring and enforcement, ensuring that ecosystem services are not compromised by competing interests.

Economic valuation strengthens the integration of ecosystem services by demonstrating their financial significance. For example, the cooling effects of urban trees can be quantified in terms of reduced energy costs, while wetlands can be valued based on their flood protection capacity. By translating ecological benefits into monetary terms, valuation helps justify investments in green infrastructure and informs cost-benefit analyses. However, valuation should complement rather than replace recognition of the intrinsic and cultural values of ecosystems, ensuring a holistic approach.

Ecosystem services provide a powerful lens for rethinking urban planning. By considering the benefits that nature delivers, cities can design infrastructure and policies that enhance resilience, reduce risks, and improve well-being. Green infrastructure, urban greening, and ecological restoration demonstrate how services can be integrated into the urban fabric. Embedding ecosystem services into planning ensures that cities are better prepared to face challenges such as climate change, population growth, and environmental degradation, creating sustainable and livable urban futures.

Chapter 6: Governance and Policy Frameworks

Ecosystem restoration requires more than ecological knowledge and technical solutions; it depends on governance systems and policy frameworks that create the conditions for long-term success. Effective governance determines how decisions are made, who participates, and how responsibilities and benefits are shared. Policies at local, national, and international levels establish the legal, institutional, and financial mechanisms that enable restoration to be scaled and sustained. Without supportive governance and coherent policies, restoration efforts risk being fragmented, short-lived, or inequitable. This chapter examines the governance structures and policy instruments that shape restoration, emphasizing accountability, inclusivity, and cross-sectoral coordination.

Institutional Arrangements for Restoration

Institutional arrangements are the frameworks of policies, organizations, laws, and practices that shape how restoration initiatives are designed, implemented, and monitored. Because ecosystem restoration requires coordination across multiple scales— local, national, and global—it is not only an ecological task but also an institutional challenge. Effective restoration depends on aligning diverse actors, creating supportive governance structures, and ensuring that responsibilities and resources are distributed in ways that enable long-term success. Institutions provide the rules and mechanisms that determine how decisions are made, who participates, and how benefits and costs are shared.

At the national level, governments play a central role in establishing policies and legal frameworks for restoration. Ministries of environment, forestry, agriculture, water, and planning are often responsible for developing regulations that protect ecosystems and create incentives for recovery. National restoration policies typically set targets, allocate budgets, and provide guidelines for implementation. Legal instruments, such as environmental protection acts, land-use regulations, and biodiversity laws, establish rights and responsibilities for both public and private actors. These frameworks create an enabling environment in which restoration can be scaled up and sustained.

Decentralization has become a prominent feature of institutional arrangements for restoration. In many countries, local governments are responsible for implementing national policies and tailoring them to regional contexts. Decentralized arrangements allow for greater flexibility and responsiveness to local ecological and social conditions. They also provide opportunities for community participation in planning and decision-making. However, decentralization requires clear mandates, adequate capacity, and financial support; otherwise, local authorities may struggle to fulfill their roles effectively. Strong coordination between national and local institutions is therefore essential.

International agreements and organizations also play a critical role. Frameworks such as the United Nations Decade on Ecosystem Restoration, the Convention on Biological Diversity, and the Ramsar Convention on Wetlands set global priorities and mobilize resources. These agreements encourage countries to commit to restoration targets, share best practices, and report progress. International financial institutions, including the Global Environment Facility and the Green Climate Fund, provide funding for large-scale restoration projects. By aligning national policies with international commitments, institutional arrangements ensure coherence and access to global support.

Non-governmental organizations (NGOs) and civil society are key actors in restoration efforts. NGOs often serve as intermediaries between governments and local communities, providing technical expertise, mobilizing resources, and advocating for ecological priorities. Civil society organizations engage in awareness-raising, monitoring, and grassroots initiatives that complement formal institutional frameworks. Their ability to innovate and adapt makes them valuable partners in restoration, particularly in areas where government capacity is limited. Institutional arrangements that recognize and integrate the contributions of NGOs and civil society strengthen overall governance.

Private sector engagement is increasingly recognized as essential for restoration. Businesses affect ecosystems through land use, resource extraction, and supply chains, but they also have the potential to support restoration through investment, innovation, and corporate responsibility initiatives. Institutional arrangements can create mechanisms such as public-private partnerships, certification schemes, and payment for ecosystem services to encourage private sector participation. Clear rules and incentives ensure that businesses contribute to restoration goals while aligning ecological outcomes with economic interests.

Financing is a critical dimension of institutional arrangements. Restoration requires sustained investment in planning, labor, monitoring, and maintenance. Public funding alone is rarely sufficient, making it necessary to combine sources such as government budgets, international aid, private finance, and community contributions. Innovative financial mechanisms—such as green bonds, trust funds, and carbon markets—provide long-term support. Institutions must ensure that financing arrangements are transparent, equitable, and aligned with restoration objectives. Without reliable funding, even well-designed projects risk failure.

Institutional capacity and knowledge systems underpin effective restoration. Institutions require skilled personnel, technical expertise, and access to data to design and implement restoration strategies. Universities, research institutes, and extension services contribute by generating scientific knowledge, developing monitoring methods, and training practitioners. Integrating traditional and local knowledge further enriches restoration practices, ensuring they are culturally relevant and socially acceptable. Institutional arrangements that support knowledge exchange and capacity building strengthen the ability of societies to manage restoration at scale.

Accountability and monitoring mechanisms are essential to ensure that institutional arrangements deliver results. Restoration is a long-term process, and institutions must track progress, evaluate outcomes, and adjust strategies as conditions change. Monitoring systems provide transparency, allowing stakeholders to assess whether resources are used effectively and whether ecological and social goals are being met. Independent oversight, citizen participation, and reporting to international bodies enhance accountability. By embedding monitoring within institutional frameworks, restoration initiatives remain adaptive and credible.

Institutional arrangements for restoration must also address equity and inclusion. Restoration can affect land rights, access to resources, and distribution of benefits. Institutions must ensure that vulnerable groups, including indigenous peoples, women, and marginalized communities, are included in decision-making and receive fair benefits from restoration. Participatory governance mechanisms create opportunities for diverse voices to shape restoration agendas, enhancing legitimacy and sustainability. Equity considerations not only uphold social justice but also increase the likelihood that restoration efforts will be maintained over the long term.

Institutional arrangements provide the foundation on which restoration efforts are built. By establishing supportive policies, coordinating actors across scales, mobilizing resources, and ensuring accountability, institutions enable ecosystems to recover and thrive. Effective arrangements integrate government, civil society, the private sector, and local communities into a cohesive framework that balances ecological, social, and economic goals. Through strong institutions, restoration can move beyond isolated projects to become a transformative force for sustainability and resilience.

National and International Policy Instruments

Policy instruments at both national and international levels are crucial for advancing ecosystem restoration. They provide the legal, financial, and institutional frameworks that guide how restoration is planned, financed, and implemented. Without clear and supportive policy instruments, restoration efforts risk remaining fragmented, underfunded, and short-lived. By aligning policies with ecological, social, and economic priorities, governments and international organizations create the enabling environment needed to scale up restoration and ensure long-term sustainability.

At the national level, legal frameworks often form the backbone of restoration policy. Environmental protection laws, forestry acts, land-use regulations, and biodiversity strategies establish rights and responsibilities for governments, private landowners, and communities. These frameworks typically set restoration targets, regulate land management, and enforce penalties for environmental damage. For example, national laws may mandate reforestation on cleared lands, protect wetlands from drainage, or require compensation for habitat loss. Embedding restoration in legislation ensures continuity beyond political cycles and provides accountability mechanisms.

National strategies and plans further operationalize legal frameworks. Many countries have developed national restoration strategies that outline priorities, timelines, and funding mechanisms. These strategies often integrate restoration into broader agendas, such as climate change adaptation, sustainable development, and rural development. Incorporating restoration into national development plans ensures that ecological goals align with economic and social objectives. Cross-sector integration—linking restoration with agriculture, water, energy, and urban planning—strengthens coherence and avoids conflicting policies.

Economic instruments at the national level play a significant role in incentivizing restoration. Governments use tools such as subsidies, tax incentives, and payments for ecosystem services to encourage landowners and businesses to invest in restoration. For example, subsidies for reforestation projects or tax reductions for conservation easements create financial motivation for private actors. Payments for ecosystem services compensate landowners for activities that enhance water quality, sequester carbon, or protect biodiversity.

These instruments align economic interests with ecological outcomes, making restoration financially viable.

Internationally, policy instruments provide frameworks for cooperation, funding, and knowledge exchange. The CBD is one of the most important, with its Aichi Targets and subsequent Kunming-Montreal Global Biodiversity Framework setting ambitious goals for ecosystem restoration and protection. The United Nations Convention to Combat Desertification (UNCCD) supports restoration through commitments to achieve land degradation neutrality. The Paris Agreement under the United Nations Framework Convention on Climate Change (UNFCCC) also recognizes restoration as a key strategy for climate mitigation and adaptation. These international agreements create binding or voluntary commitments that encourage countries to prioritize restoration.

The Ramsar Convention on Wetlands is another influential instrument, focusing specifically on wetland conservation and restoration. By designating wetlands of international importance, countries commit to their protection and sustainable management. Similarly, regional agreements, such as the European Union's Habitats Directive or the African Union's Great Green Wall initiative, provide frameworks tailored to specific ecological and social contexts. These instruments demonstrate how international cooperation can address shared challenges while respecting regional diversity.

Funding mechanisms established by international organizations are critical for scaling restoration. Institutions such as the GEF, the GCF, and the World Bank provide financial resources for large-scale projects. These funds often support developing countries, where restoration needs are high but financial capacity is limited. International financing is frequently tied to national commitments under global agreements, linking policy with resource allocation. Access to international finance helps bridge gaps in domestic budgets and accelerates implementation.

Policy instruments also facilitate knowledge exchange and capacity building. International initiatives such as the United Nations Decade on Ecosystem Restoration (2021–2030) create platforms for sharing best practices, advancing scientific research, and building technical skills. Networks of practitioners, policymakers, and researchers promote collaboration across borders, enabling countries to learn from one another's experiences. These initiatives highlight the role of policy instruments not only in regulation and funding but also in fostering innovation and collaboration.

Monitoring and reporting are embedded in many international policy instruments. Countries are often required to submit progress reports on restoration commitments, ensuring accountability and transparency. Global databases and monitoring systems, supported by satellite imagery and remote sensing, track ecosystem changes and evaluate policy effectiveness. Reporting obligations encourage countries to collect data, evaluate performance, and refine strategies. By standardizing monitoring frameworks, international instruments ensure comparability and enable collective assessment of progress toward global goals.

Equity and inclusion are increasingly emphasized in policy instruments. Restoration policies at both national and international levels recognize the importance of involving indigenous peoples, local communities, and marginalized groups. Instruments encourage participatory governance, safeguard land rights, and ensure fair distribution of benefits. International frameworks highlight the role of traditional knowledge and community-based approaches, reinforcing that restoration must be socially just as well as ecologically effective.

National and international policy instruments together form the scaffolding that supports ecosystem restoration. National laws, strategies, and economic incentives provide the foundation for local implementation, while international agreements, financing, and monitoring frameworks create global coherence and momentum. Effective integration of these instruments ensures that restoration is not an isolated activity but a mainstream component of development, climate, and biodiversity agendas. By strengthening legal, financial, and institutional support at all levels, policy instruments enable restoration to achieve the scale and impact needed to address today's environmental challenges.

Multi-Level Governance and Stakeholder Engagement

Ecosystem restoration is a complex endeavor that involves multiple actors, interests, and scales of governance. From local communities and municipalities to national governments and international organizations, diverse stakeholders influence how restoration is planned, financed, and implemented. Multi-level governance provides the framework for coordinating actions across these scales, ensuring that restoration policies are coherent, inclusive, and effective. At the same time, stakeholder engagement ensures that those directly affected by restoration initiatives have a voice in decision-making and share in the benefits. Together, multi-level governance and stakeholder engagement create the enabling environment for sustainable and equitable restoration.

Multi-level governance refers to the vertical and horizontal coordination among institutions operating at different levels of authority. Vertically, it links local, regional, national, and international institutions. For example, local restoration projects may align with national biodiversity strategies, which in turn reflect commitments under international conventions. Horizontally, governance involves collaboration across sectors such as agriculture, forestry, water, and urban planning, recognizing that ecosystems cut across administrative boundaries. Without multi-level coordination, restoration risks becoming fragmented, with conflicting objectives and inefficient use of resources.

At the local level, governance structures are critical because restoration often takes place on community-managed lands, farms, and municipal territories. Local authorities, community organizations, and indigenous groups play direct roles in planning and implementing restoration. Their involvement ensures that strategies are tailored to local ecological conditions and cultural values. Local governance also provides opportunities for experimentation and innovation, allowing restoration methods to be tested and adapted before scaling up. However, local institutions often face resource and capacity constraints, making support from higher levels of governance essential.

Regional and national governments provide the policy frameworks and financial resources needed to support restoration at scale. National biodiversity strategies, land-use policies, and environmental regulations establish the enabling conditions for local initiatives. Regional governments often act as intermediaries, translating national policies into regional priorities and coordinating across municipalities. They may also manage transboundary ecosystems such as watersheds, forests, or rangelands that span administrative boundaries. By bridging local and national levels, regional governance ensures coherence and integration.

International governance provides overarching frameworks that set restoration priorities and mobilize resources. Agreements such as the Convention on Biological Diversity, the United Nations Convention to Combat Desertification, and the Paris Agreement establish global goals that influence national strategies. International organizations and funding mechanisms provide technical support and financial resources, particularly to countries with limited capacity. Multi-level governance ensures that these global frameworks are translated into meaningful local action while reflecting the realities on the ground.

Stakeholder engagement complements multi-level governance by ensuring that diverse perspectives and interests are included in restoration. Stakeholders include governments, NGOs, businesses, scientists, landowners, indigenous peoples, and local communities. Engaging these groups in planning and decision-making enhances legitimacy, fosters trust, and increases the likelihood of long-term success. Participatory processes allow stakeholders to influence project design, identify priorities, and resolve conflicts. By creating platforms for dialogue and collaboration, stakeholder engagement helps balance competing interests and ensures equitable outcomes.

Community participation is particularly important for restoration because local people are often the custodians of ecosystems and bear the costs and benefits of interventions. Involving communities in decision-making builds ownership and strengthens stewardship. Community-based monitoring, for example, empowers local people to track ecological changes and adapt management practices. Traditional knowledge held by indigenous peoples and local communities enriches restoration approaches, offering insights into sustainable land management and species interactions. Institutional arrangements that respect land rights and provide equitable benefits further reinforce community engagement.

The private sector is an increasingly important stakeholder in restoration. Businesses influence ecosystems through their operations and supply chains, but they can also contribute resources, technology, and innovation. Engaging the private sector requires creating incentives for sustainable practices, such as certification schemes, payment for ecosystem services, or corporate social responsibility initiatives. Public-private partnerships are one mechanism for aligning business interests with restoration goals. By involving the private sector as stakeholders, governance frameworks expand the financial and technical capacity for restoration.

NGOs and civil society organizations also play vital roles in stakeholder engagement. They act as advocates, intermediaries, and implementers, often bridging gaps between governments and communities. NGOs bring technical expertise, mobilize funding, and promote awareness, while civil society groups represent grassroots perspectives. Their involvement ensures that restoration initiatives are inclusive, socially just, and responsive to local needs. Governance frameworks that recognize the contributions of NGOs and civil society create stronger, more resilient restoration systems.

Effective multi-level governance and stakeholder engagement require mechanisms for coordination, communication, and accountability. Multi-stakeholder platforms, advisory councils, and participatory planning processes provide spaces for dialogue and negotiation. Monitoring and reporting frameworks ensure that commitments are met and allow stakeholders to evaluate progress. Adaptive governance, which emphasizes learning and flexibility, enables institutions to respond to changing ecological and social conditions. By embedding accountability and adaptability, governance systems remain relevant and effective over time.

Multi-level governance and stakeholder engagement are essential pillars of ecosystem restoration. Governance structures link local action with national policies and global commitments, ensuring coherence across scales. Stakeholder engagement ensures that diverse voices are heard, benefits are shared, and solutions are socially acceptable. Together, they provide the foundation for restoration efforts that are inclusive, equitable, and sustainable. By coordinating institutions and empowering stakeholders, societies can achieve restoration outcomes that not only heal ecosystems but also strengthen resilience and human well-being.

Rights-Based Approaches and Indigenous Knowledge

Rights-based approaches to ecosystem restoration emphasize that ecological recovery must go hand in hand with protecting human rights, particularly those of indigenous peoples and local communities who are often the custodians of natural resources. These approaches recognize that restoration cannot succeed if it undermines the rights of people who depend on ecosystems for their survival and cultural identity. Instead, restoration should be designed and implemented in ways that empower communities, secure tenure, and respect cultural traditions, while also advancing ecological sustainability.

At the core of rights-based approaches is the principle of participation. Restoration initiatives must involve affected communities in all stages of decision-making, from planning and implementation to monitoring and benefit-sharing. Participation goes beyond consultation, ensuring that communities have genuine influence over outcomes. Inclusive processes respect the rights of people to be heard, to give or withhold consent, and to shape the priorities of restoration. Free, prior, and informed consent (FPIC) is particularly important when projects affect indigenous lands and territories, guaranteeing that communities have the right to make decisions without coercion.

Land tenure security is another cornerstone of rights-based restoration. In many parts of the world, indigenous peoples and local communities lack formal recognition of their rights to land and resources, leaving them vulnerable to displacement when restoration projects are introduced. Without secure tenure, restoration efforts risk exacerbating inequality and conflict. Rights-based approaches prioritize clarifying and securing land rights, often through legal recognition, community mapping, and land registration. When communities are confident in their rights, they are more likely to invest in sustainable practices and long-term stewardship of restored ecosystems.

Indigenous knowledge is a critical element of rights-based restoration, offering insights into ecological processes, resource management, and adaptation strategies honed over generations. Traditional practices such as rotational farming, controlled burning, water harvesting, and sacred site protection often align with ecological principles and contribute to ecosystem resilience. Incorporating indigenous knowledge enriches restoration strategies, ensuring they are culturally relevant and ecologically effective. Collaboration between scientists and indigenous communities can generate hybrid knowledge systems that combine traditional wisdom with modern science for more innovative and resilient solutions.

Cultural values and spiritual connections to land are integral to indigenous perspectives on restoration. For many indigenous peoples, ecosystems are not just sources of resources but are also central to identity, spirituality, and worldviews. Rights-based approaches recognize these values by respecting sacred sites, cultural landscapes, and customary practices. Restoration that supports cultural renewal—such as reviving traditional land management or reintroducing culturally important species—strengthens both ecological and cultural resilience. In this way, restoration becomes not only a technical process but also a cultural and spiritual renewal.

Benefit-sharing is another important dimension of rights-based restoration. Restoration projects often generate benefits such as jobs, ecosystem services, carbon credits, and improved livelihoods. Ensuring that these benefits are equitably shared with local and indigenous communities is essential for justice and sustainability. Mechanisms such as community funds, revenue-sharing agreements, or co-management arrangements help distribute benefits fairly. Transparent agreements and participatory governance structures build trust and accountability, ensuring that restoration contributes to poverty reduction and social equity.

International frameworks provide strong support for rights-based approaches and the inclusion of indigenous knowledge. Instruments such as the United Nations Declaration on the Rights of Indigenous Peoples (UNDRIP), International Labour Organization Convention 169, and the CBD emphasize the rights of indigenous peoples to participate in decisions affecting their lands and resources. The UN Decade on Ecosystem Restoration (2021–2030) also highlights the central role of indigenous knowledge and rights in achieving restoration goals. These frameworks create political and legal backing for embedding rights-based principles in restoration practice.

Challenges remain in operationalizing rights-based approaches. Power imbalances, weak governance, and lack of resources can limit the effective participation of marginalized groups. Conflicts between national development priorities and local rights may also arise, particularly where large-scale restoration intersects with extractive industries or infrastructure development. Addressing these challenges requires strong safeguards, transparent governance, and capacity building for both communities and institutions. Strengthening indigenous organizations and supporting legal advocacy are vital for ensuring that rights are upheld.

Monitoring and accountability mechanisms are essential for ensuring that rights-based restoration delivers on its promises. Independent oversight, grievance mechanisms, and participatory monitoring enable communities to hold governments and organizations accountable. Tracking not only ecological outcomes but also social and rights-based indicators ensures that restoration contributes to both environmental and human well-being. By embedding rights into monitoring frameworks, restoration projects can demonstrate that they respect and uphold social justice alongside ecological recovery.

Rights-based approaches and indigenous knowledge enrich ecosystem restoration by ensuring that it is socially just, culturally relevant, and ecologically resilient. Recognizing and protecting the rights of communities, integrating traditional knowledge, and ensuring equitable benefits transform restoration into a collaborative process that empowers people as much as it heals ecosystems. These approaches highlight that sustainability is not only about ecological balance but also about justice, inclusion, and respect for the deep connections between people and the natural world.

Chapter 7: Financing Ecosystem Restoration

Financing ecosystem restoration is critical for transforming local projects into large-scale, lasting initiatives. Restoration demands upfront investment in planning, infrastructure, and monitoring, while ecological and social benefits may take decades to fully emerge. Stable and diversified funding sources are therefore essential to sustain momentum and achieve meaningful outcomes. Embedding restoration in financial systems ensures it is recognized as a long-term investment in natural capital rather than an isolated cost. This chapter explores public, private, and innovative financing mechanisms, analyzing opportunities and challenges to build sustainable, equitable, and scalable systems that link ecological recovery with economic development.

Public and Private Financing Mechanisms

Financing is one of the most critical components of ecosystem restoration, determining whether initiatives can move from small-scale projects to large-scale, long-term programs. Restoration often requires significant upfront investment in planning, labor, infrastructure, and monitoring, while ecological and social benefits may take years to materialize. Public and private financing mechanisms provide the resources needed to bridge this gap. By combining the strengths of both sectors—public sector stability and private sector innovation—restoration financing can be scaled and diversified to meet global needs.

Public financing mechanisms remain the foundation for restoration in many countries. Governments allocate funds through national budgets, often channeled via ministries of environment, forestry, agriculture, or water. These allocations may support national restoration programs, subsidies for landowners, or infrastructure projects such as watershed rehabilitation. International aid and development assistance also play a major role, particularly in developing countries where domestic resources are limited.

Multilateral institutions such as the World Bank, the GEF, and the GCF provide grants and concessional loans to support large-scale restoration projects that align with climate, biodiversity, and development goals.

Tax incentives and subsidies are widely used public instruments to encourage restoration. For instance, landowners may receive tax breaks for reforesting degraded land or conserving wetlands. Subsidies can cover the costs of seedlings, fencing, or technical support, reducing barriers for farmers and communities to participate in restoration. Payment for ecosystem services (PES) schemes, often publicly funded, provide direct financial rewards to land managers who undertake restoration activities that deliver benefits such as improved water quality, carbon sequestration, or biodiversity conservation. These mechanisms link ecological outcomes with financial incentives, aligning private behavior with public goals.

Private financing mechanisms are increasingly important as restoration is mainstreamed into business and investment strategies. Companies are recognizing the financial risks posed by ecosystem degradation, such as supply chain disruptions, water scarcity, and reputational damage. In response, businesses are investing in restoration as part of corporate sustainability strategies, carbon neutrality commitments, or risk management plans. Private investors are also entering the space, viewing restoration as an opportunity to generate financial returns while delivering environmental and social benefits.

Impact investment is one key avenue for private financing. Impact investors seek both financial returns and measurable positive outcomes, making restoration an attractive sector. Investments may support projects such as reforestation, regenerative agriculture, or mangrove restoration, where ecological benefits are quantifiable. Green bonds and sustainability-linked loans are also becoming popular instruments. These financial products raise capital for projects with environmental objectives, offering investors stable returns while funding restoration. The global green bond market has grown rapidly, with billions of dollars mobilized for projects related to nature-based solutions.

Carbon finance is another major private mechanism driving restoration. Under voluntary and compliance carbon markets, companies purchase carbon credits to offset emissions, providing revenue for projects that sequester carbon through reforestation, afforestation, or soil restoration. High-quality carbon projects not only capture carbon but also generate co-benefits such as biodiversity conservation and community development. Standards such as the Verified Carbon Standard (VCS) or Gold Standard ensure credibility and transparency, building investor confidence. As demand for carbon credits grows, restoration projects are increasingly positioned as valuable assets in carbon markets.

Blended finance combines public and private resources to reduce risk and attract investment in restoration. Public funds, including grants or concessional loans, can be used to de-risk projects by covering early-stage costs, offering guarantees, or absorbing initial losses. This reduces perceived risks for private investors, encouraging them to participate. For example, governments or multilateral institutions may fund feasibility studies, while private investors provide capital for implementation once risks are better understood. Blended finance leverages limited public funds to mobilize much larger private investment, making it a powerful tool for scaling restoration.

Community-based financing mechanisms also play an important role. Cooperatives, savings groups, and local enterprises often pool resources for small-scale restoration initiatives. Microfinance institutions may provide loans for activities such as agroforestry, organic farming, or watershed management. These localized mechanisms empower communities, promote ownership, and ensure that restoration aligns with local priorities. While smaller in scale, community-based financing complements larger public and private mechanisms, particularly by reaching marginalized groups and supporting grassroots initiatives.

Effective financing requires robust governance and monitoring frameworks. Investors and donors need confidence that funds are used effectively and that ecological outcomes are achieved. Transparent reporting, accountability mechanisms, and independent verification strengthen trust in financing arrangements. Clear land tenure and rights are also essential, as they reduce risks of conflict and ensure that benefits flow to those undertaking restoration. By addressing governance challenges, financing mechanisms can attract more capital and ensure equitable distribution of benefits.

Scaling restoration finance also depends on aligning it with broader policy and economic frameworks. National policies that integrate restoration into climate strategies, development plans, and agricultural programs create demand for financing. International agreements such as the Paris Agreement and the Convention on Biological Diversity generate political momentum, which in turn mobilizes funding. Financial institutions are increasingly adopting environmental, social, and governance (ESG) criteria, channeling investment toward sustainable projects. By embedding restoration in policy and finance systems, funding becomes more predictable and long-term.

Public and private financing mechanisms together create a diverse portfolio of options for supporting ecosystem restoration. Public financing provides stability, equity, and scale, while private financing introduces innovation, efficiency, and additional resources. Blended approaches and community-based mechanisms further enhance inclusivity and effectiveness. By combining these mechanisms and embedding them in strong governance frameworks, societies can mobilize the billions of dollars needed to restore ecosystems at scale. Financing is not just about resources but also about creating the incentives, structures, and trust necessary to ensure that restoration is sustainable and equitable.

Payment for Ecosystem Services and Market-Based Tools

PES and related market-based tools are mechanisms that assign economic value to the benefits nature provides, creating financial incentives for conservation and restoration. These tools recognize that ecosystems deliver vital services such as clean water, carbon sequestration, biodiversity, and cultural values, yet these benefits are often undervalued in conventional markets. By linking ecological outcomes with economic transactions, PES and market-based approaches encourage landowners, communities, and businesses to manage ecosystems sustainably while ensuring that those who bear the costs of stewardship are fairly compensated.

The concept of PES rests on the principle of beneficiaries paying for the services they receive. For example, a downstream city that relies on clean water may pay upstream landowners to maintain forests or wetlands that filter and regulate water flows. Similarly, companies seeking to offset carbon emissions may fund reforestation projects that capture carbon dioxide. These arrangements align ecological and economic incentives, ensuring that protecting ecosystems is not only an ethical choice but also a financially viable one. PES schemes typically involve four key elements: clearly defined services, identifiable providers and beneficiaries, a financial transfer mechanism, and measurable outcomes.

Water-related PES schemes are among the most common. Many cities have established programs where water utilities or municipalities pay upstream land managers to maintain forests, reduce erosion, and limit agricultural runoff. These actions protect watersheds, reduce treatment costs, and ensure a reliable supply of clean water. Examples include watershed funds that pool contributions from multiple beneficiaries, such as industries, households, and governments, to finance restoration and conservation. Such models highlight how PES can create collective responsibility for safeguarding ecosystem services that support urban and rural communities alike.

Carbon markets provide another major application of market-based tools for ecosystem services. Under voluntary and compliance systems, carbon credits are generated by projects that sequester carbon through activities such as afforestation, reforestation, peatland restoration, or improved soil management. These credits are then sold to companies or governments seeking to offset emissions. Standards such as the VCS and Gold Standard ensure the credibility of carbon projects by requiring rigorous monitoring and verification. Carbon markets create significant financial opportunities for restoration, while simultaneously contributing to climate mitigation and biodiversity co-benefits.

Biodiversity offsets represent a market-based approach designed to compensate for ecological damage caused by development. Under these schemes, developers are required to restore, protect, or enhance biodiversity in one area to offset impacts elsewhere. Ideally, offsets are designed to achieve "no net loss" or even a net gain of biodiversity. Market mechanisms, such as biodiversity credit trading, enable developers to purchase credits from certified restoration or conservation projects. While controversial, these tools have gained traction as a way to integrate ecological considerations into economic decision-making and to channel investment toward restoration.

Agri-environmental schemes are another example of PES in practice. Farmers and landowners receive payments for adopting practices that enhance ecosystem services, such as maintaining hedgerows, restoring wetlands, or practicing regenerative agriculture. These payments often come from governments or international donors but are increasingly supported by private supply chains seeking sustainable sourcing. By rewarding environmentally friendly practices, agri-environmental schemes integrate production and conservation, demonstrating how market-based tools can support both food security and ecosystem restoration.

For PES and market-based tools to succeed, governance and institutional frameworks are critical. Clearly defined property rights and land tenure are essential to determine who has the authority to provide services and receive payments. Transparent rules, accountability mechanisms, and stakeholder participation help ensure that PES schemes are equitable and effective. Without strong governance, there is a risk of elite capture, exclusion of marginalized groups, or ineffective delivery of ecological benefits. Institutions must therefore design PES with safeguards that prioritize social justice alongside ecological outcomes.

Financing mechanisms play an important role in sustaining PES schemes. Trust funds, revolving funds, and blended finance arrangements provide stable, long-term resources for payments. Public funds often cover start-up costs, while private contributions sustain programs over time. Innovative financing, such as green bonds or insurance-linked instruments, is increasingly being applied to PES, expanding the pool of capital available for restoration. By diversifying funding sources, PES can move beyond donor dependency and achieve greater financial resilience.

Community participation and equity are central to the success of PES. Many schemes take place in areas where indigenous peoples and local communities depend on ecosystems for their livelihoods. Ensuring that these groups are recognized as service providers, that their rights are protected, and that they receive fair compensation is essential. Participatory design strengthens trust, incorporates traditional knowledge, and increases the likelihood of long-term sustainability. When communities see tangible benefits—whether in cash payments, improved infrastructure, or enhanced livelihoods— they are more likely to support restoration and conservation.

Monitoring and evaluation underpin the credibility of PES and market-based tools. Beneficiaries must be assured that payments result in real and measurable ecological improvements. Indicators such as water quality, carbon sequestration, or biodiversity levels provide evidence of outcomes. Advances in remote sensing, environmental DNA, and digital monitoring platforms enhance the ability to track ecosystem services accurately and cost-effectively. Transparent reporting strengthens accountability, builds trust, and attracts further investment.

Payment for ecosystem services and market-based tools demonstrate how aligning economic incentives with ecological goals can drive restoration at scale. By creating financial value for clean water, carbon storage, biodiversity, and other services, these mechanisms make conservation and restoration attractive to landowners, communities, and businesses. When embedded in strong governance frameworks and designed with equity in mind, PES can transform restoration from a cost to an opportunity, ensuring that ecosystems and societies thrive together.

Green Bonds and Innovative Financing Instruments

Ecosystem restoration requires significant investment, often over long timeframes before ecological and social benefits fully materialize. Traditional funding sources, such as government budgets and donor grants, remain important but are insufficient to meet the scale of restoration needed globally. Innovative financing instruments, including green bonds, sustainability-linked loans, blended finance, and other novel mechanisms, are emerging as powerful tools to mobilize capital for restoration. These instruments leverage financial markets, private investment, and creative partnerships to bridge funding gaps and ensure that ecological recovery is both scalable and sustainable.

Green bonds are one of the most widely used instruments for financing environmental projects. They are debt securities issued to raise capital for projects with positive environmental impacts, such as reforestation, wetland rehabilitation, or watershed restoration. Investors purchase these bonds with the assurance that proceeds will be used exclusively for green purposes. To ensure credibility, issuers typically follow guidelines such as the Green Bond Principles established by the International Capital Market Association, which require transparency, reporting, and independent verification. Green bonds appeal to institutional investors seeking stable returns while meeting ESG objectives, thereby channeling large volumes of capital into restoration efforts.

Sustainability-linked bonds and loans expand on this model by linking financing terms directly to sustainability performance. Unlike green bonds, which earmark proceeds for specific projects, sustainability-linked instruments adjust interest rates or repayment terms based on the borrower's achievement of agreed environmental targets. For example, a company could secure lower financing costs if it meets targets for reforesting degraded land or reducing biodiversity impacts in its supply chain. This model incentivizes organizations to embed restoration objectives within broader operations, aligning financial benefits with ecological performance.

Blended finance mechanisms combine public and private resources to de-risk restoration investments. Public funds, philanthropic capital, or concessional loans are used to absorb initial risks, making projects more attractive to private investors. By lowering perceived risks, blended finance unlocks private capital for projects that might otherwise be overlooked due to long time horizons or uncertain returns. Restoration funds structured with layered financing, where different investors assume different levels of risk, are becoming more common. These arrangements leverage limited public funding to attract much larger private contributions, expanding the pool of resources available for restoration.

Insurance-linked instruments also present innovative opportunities for financing restoration. Parametric insurance, for instance, can provide payouts when environmental thresholds are crossed, such as extreme storms or droughts, enabling rapid recovery and restoration efforts. Some initiatives are exploring reef and mangrove insurance, where premiums paid by governments, businesses, or communities fund restoration of natural coastal defenses. By linking financial resilience with ecological resilience, insurance-based instruments align the interests of insurers, policymakers, and ecosystems.

Carbon markets continue to be a significant driver of restoration finance. Verified carbon credits generated from reforestation, afforestation, or peatland restoration projects are sold to companies or governments seeking to offset emissions. Revenues from these credits finance ongoing restoration activities, creating a performance-based funding model. Innovations within carbon markets, such as biodiversity credits or bundled credits that combine carbon and other ecosystem services, are expanding opportunities to monetize ecological benefits beyond carbon sequestration alone. These emerging markets help diversify revenue streams and increase financial sustainability for restoration projects.

Crowdfunding and community investment platforms represent another innovative mechanism, particularly for smaller-scale or grassroots initiatives. By pooling contributions from individuals, communities, or philanthropic supporters, these platforms finance localized restoration projects that may not attract institutional investors. Digital platforms enhance transparency by providing real-time updates on ecological outcomes, building trust and accountability. While smaller in scale compared to green bonds or blended finance, community-driven instruments democratize restoration finance and strengthen public engagement.

Effective governance is critical to the credibility and success of innovative financing instruments. Transparency, accountability, and clear monitoring systems ensure that funds are used appropriately and that ecological outcomes are achieved. Independent verification, robust reporting standards, and alignment with international frameworks such as the Sustainable Development Goals enhance investor confidence. Without strong safeguards, there is a risk of "greenwashing," where funds are labeled as green but deliver little or no environmental benefit. Strengthening governance frameworks builds trust and ensures that innovative finance delivers genuine restoration outcomes.

Equity considerations must also be embedded in financing models. Restoration projects often take place on lands managed by indigenous peoples and local communities. Financing mechanisms should ensure that these groups are recognized as key stakeholders and benefit fairly from investments. Participatory design, revenue-sharing agreements, and safeguards for land and resource rights ensure that financing contributes to social as well as ecological goals. By integrating equity into financing instruments, restoration becomes a pathway to inclusive development as well as environmental sustainability.

Green bonds and innovative financing instruments represent a paradigm shift in how restoration is funded. By mobilizing private capital, aligning financial incentives with ecological outcomes, and diversifying funding sources, these instruments help close the gap between ambition and implementation. When designed with transparency, equity, and robust monitoring, they can scale restoration to the levels required to address global challenges. Through innovation in finance, restoration is no longer viewed solely as a cost but as an investment in resilience, sustainability, and shared prosperity.

Aligning Restoration with Economic Development

Ecosystem restoration is often viewed as an environmental objective, but it also has significant implications for economic development. Healthy ecosystems provide essential goods and services that underpin agriculture, industry, energy production, and human well-being. When ecosystems are degraded, these services decline, leading to economic losses through reduced productivity, increased disaster risks, and higher costs for infrastructure and health. Aligning restoration with economic development ensures that ecological recovery not only benefits biodiversity but also strengthens livelihoods, supports inclusive growth, and contributes to national and global development goals.

One of the most direct ways restoration supports economic development is by sustaining agriculture and food security. Restored soils, wetlands, and watersheds improve water availability, nutrient cycling, and resilience to climate variability, all of which are vital for agricultural productivity. Agroforestry, regenerative agriculture, and soil restoration projects increase yields while reducing dependence on chemical inputs. These practices enhance long-term productivity, reduce costs for farmers, and contribute to rural development. By integrating restoration into agricultural systems,

96

countries can secure food supplies while diversifying rural economies and creating new income streams.

Restoration also contributes to economic development by reducing risks and costs associated with natural disasters. Healthy ecosystems such as mangroves, wetlands, and forests act as natural buffers against floods, storms, droughts, and landslides. By reducing disaster damage, restoration lowers costs for governments, businesses, and households. For example, restoring coastal ecosystems reduces the need for expensive seawalls while protecting fisheries and tourism industries. In economic terms, investing in restoration often yields higher returns than investing solely in engineered infrastructure, making it a cost-effective strategy for risk reduction and development planning.

Employment generation is another critical link between restoration and economic development. Restoration projects are labor-intensive, involving activities such as tree planting, soil management, invasive species removal, and monitoring. These activities create jobs, particularly in rural and marginalized areas where alternative employment opportunities may be limited. Beyond short-term jobs, restoration can stimulate long-term economic sectors such as ecotourism, sustainable forestry, and ecosystem services markets. By investing in restoration, governments and businesses can promote green jobs and strengthen inclusive economic growth.

Restoration also enhances water security, which is central to economic development. Healthy watersheds regulate water flows, reduce sedimentation, and improve water quality, ensuring reliable supplies for agriculture, industry, and households. Clean and consistent water access reduces costs for water treatment and energy production, while supporting industries such as hydropower, manufacturing, and tourism. Countries that align restoration with water resource management secure critical inputs for economic activity and reduce conflicts over scarce resources. This highlights how restoration is not separate from development but integral to sustaining the natural capital on which economies depend.

Ecosystem restoration contributes to energy security and climate goals, further linking it with economic priorities. Reforestation and soil restoration sequester carbon, supporting national climate commitments and positioning countries in carbon markets. Restored ecosystems can provide renewable energy resources, such as sustainable biomass or hydropower from healthy watersheds. By contributing to low-carbon development, restoration reduces vulnerability to climate impacts and aligns with long-term economic strategies for competitiveness in a global green economy.

Tourism is another sector where restoration directly supports development. Pristine landscapes, healthy coral reefs, and biodiverse forests attract visitors, generating income and employment. Degraded ecosystems, by contrast, undermine tourism potential and reduce foreign exchange earnings. Restoration projects that rehabilitate landscapes and biodiversity can revitalize tourism industries, particularly in countries where nature-based tourism is a major contributor to GDP. Linking restoration with tourism planning creates opportunities for community involvement and equitable distribution of benefits.

Policy frameworks play a central role in aligning restoration with economic development. Governments can integrate restoration into national development plans, infrastructure projects, and sectoral policies such as agriculture, energy, and water. By embedding restoration within economic planning, policymakers ensure that ecological sustainability is treated as a driver of growth rather than a constraint. Cross-sectoral coordination is essential, as restoration affects and is affected by multiple sectors. For example, aligning agricultural subsidies with restoration goals promotes both productivity and ecological resilience.

Financing mechanisms also help connect restoration with development objectives. Green bonds, payment for ecosystem services, and blended finance instruments channel investment into projects that generate both ecological and economic benefits. By framing restoration as an investment in natural capital, these mechanisms attract capital from development banks, private investors, and international funds. This approach ensures that restoration is not seen as a cost but as a productive investment that yields economic returns.

Equity and inclusion are critical considerations when aligning restoration with development. Restoration projects must ensure that benefits flow to local communities, indigenous peoples, and marginalized groups, who are often most dependent on ecosystems and most vulnerable to degradation. Participatory approaches, fair benefit-sharing, and recognition of land rights build trust and social cohesion. By promoting inclusive development, restoration can reduce poverty and inequality while strengthening social resilience.

Aligning restoration with economic development highlights that ecological recovery and prosperity are not competing goals but mutually reinforcing. Healthy ecosystems provide the foundation for agriculture, water security, disaster resilience, climate mitigation, and tourism—all essential pillars of economic growth. Restoration creates jobs, reduces risks, and sustains natural capital, ensuring that development is sustainable in the long term. By embedding restoration into economic planning and investment, societies can pursue growth that is not only productive but also resilient, inclusive, and ecologically sound.

Chapter 8: Tools, Techniques, and Innovations

Ecosystem restoration today merges traditional knowledge with modern science and technology to address complex challenges across terrestrial, freshwater, marine, and urban systems. Advances such as soil regeneration techniques, hydrological engineering, biotechnology, and artificial intelligence are reshaping how degraded ecosystems can be restored with greater precision and efficiency. Digital monitoring tools and ecological engineering approaches enhance accountability and scalability, while innovations in biotechnology expand opportunities for resilience under climate stress. This chapter examines the tools and techniques driving effective restoration, emphasizing the integration of community knowledge with technological advances to create adaptive, inclusive, and sustainable restoration practices.

Ecological Engineering and Restoration Technologies

Ecological engineering and restoration technologies represent the practical tools and approaches used to repair degraded ecosystems and re-establish their natural functions. These methods draw from ecology, hydrology, soil science, and engineering, combining traditional ecological knowledge with modern innovations. By using science-based interventions, ecological engineering aims not only to restore biodiversity but also to enhance ecosystem services such as carbon storage, water regulation, and disaster risk reduction. As ecosystems continue to face pressures from urbanization, agriculture, and climate change, restoration technologies are becoming increasingly essential for scaling and sustaining ecological recovery.

One of the cornerstones of ecological engineering is hydrological restoration. Water is a defining factor for many ecosystems, and disruptions to natural flows are a leading cause of degradation. Techniques such as re-meandering rivers, breaching levees, and removing drainage channels allow rivers, wetlands, and floodplains to regain their natural dynamics. In urban areas, stormwater

100

management technologies—including permeable pavements, bioswales, and constructed wetlands—mimic natural processes to reduce flooding and improve water quality. These interventions restore the ecological integrity of aquatic systems while also protecting human settlements from extreme events.

Soil restoration technologies are equally critical. Degraded soils often suffer from compaction, nutrient loss, and erosion, which limit vegetation growth and ecosystem recovery. Ecological engineering approaches include biochar application, compost amendments, and microbial inoculation to rebuild soil fertility and structure. Techniques such as contour plowing, terracing, and the installation of check dams stabilize soils and reduce erosion. Advances in soil biotechnology, including engineered microbes that enhance nutrient cycling, hold promise for accelerating recovery. Restoring healthy soils underpins broader ecological functions, from carbon sequestration to water retention.

Vegetation establishment technologies are widely used in reforestation, grassland recovery, and wetland restoration. Seedling planting, direct seeding, and hydroseeding are common methods, often supported by innovations such as seed coating to improve germination and drought tolerance. Drones are increasingly used to disperse seeds across large or inaccessible areas, allowing rapid re-vegetation at scale. Assisted natural regeneration, where human interventions such as weeding and protection from grazing facilitate natural succession, is another cost-effective approach. By integrating ecological knowledge with technology, vegetation restoration enhances biodiversity while stabilizing ecosystems.

Marine and coastal restoration technologies have advanced significantly in recent years. For coral reefs, methods such as coral gardening, microfragmentation, and artificial reef structures are being deployed to accelerate recovery. Seagrass meadows are restored using transplanting and seeding techniques, often supported by underwater drones and precision mapping tools. Mangrove restoration relies on hydrological rehabilitation combined with planting native species in appropriate tidal zones. These technologies strengthen coastal resilience, protect communities from storms, and restore habitats critical for marine biodiversity.

Ecological engineering also embraces bioengineering techniques that use living materials to stabilize and restore environments. Examples include using willows or vetiver grass to control erosion on riverbanks, or coir mats and geotextiles to stabilize slopes while vegetation establishes. These solutions integrate biological and structural elements, providing both immediate protection and long-term ecological benefits. Unlike hard infrastructure such as concrete walls, bioengineering evolves over time, adapting to changing conditions while maintaining ecosystem functions.

Technology is increasingly integrated into monitoring and adaptive management of restoration. Remote sensing, drones, and geographic information systems (GIS) provide detailed data on vegetation cover, hydrology, and land use. EDNA techniques allow detection of species presence and biodiversity trends without direct observation. Automated sensors track water quality, soil moisture, and carbon fluxes in real time. These tools enable practitioners to evaluate the effectiveness of restoration interventions, refine strategies, and ensure accountability. Digital platforms also enhance community involvement by allowing citizen scientists to contribute to monitoring efforts.

Innovations in biotechnology are expanding the toolkit for restoration. Genetic techniques, such as selecting drought-resistant or pest-tolerant plant varieties, are being used to increase survival rates in reforestation. Assisted migration, where species are relocated to areas with more suitable climatic conditions, is another emerging approach. In marine systems, researchers are experimenting with breeding corals that are more resistant to heat stress and ocean acidification. While these technologies raise ethical and ecological questions, they illustrate how restoration is evolving to address the challenges of a rapidly changing world.

Collaboration between engineering disciplines and ecological science is vital for the success of restoration technologies. Infrastructure projects increasingly integrate ecological engineering principles, such as designing levees with habitat features or constructing green roofs that support biodiversity. By embedding ecological considerations into engineering, restoration contributes to both human and environmental goals. This interdisciplinary approach ensures that restoration technologies are not only technically sound but also socially acceptable and ecologically effective.

Ecological engineering and restoration technologies highlight the potential of combining natural processes with human innovation to repair damaged ecosystems. From hydrological rehabilitation and soil biotechnology to coral gardening and bioengineering, these tools enable ecosystems to recover their structure, function, and resilience. Monitoring technologies and biotechnology further enhance the ability to scale and sustain restoration. As societies seek to address biodiversity loss, climate change, and resource degradation, ecological engineering provides practical pathways for aligning environmental recovery with human well-being and development.

Digital Tools, AI, and Remote Sensing in Restoration

The integration of digital tools, artificial intelligence (AI), and remote sensing is transforming how ecosystem restoration is planned, implemented, and monitored. Restoration has historically been limited by gaps in data, difficulties in assessing ecological changes over large areas, and challenges in predicting long-term outcomes. Today, digital technologies are closing these gaps by providing unprecedented accuracy, scalability, and efficiency. They allow practitioners to monitor ecosystems in real time, model future scenarios, and optimize restoration strategies. These innovations make it possible to restore ecosystems at scales and speeds that were once unimaginable.

Remote sensing is one of the most important technologies for ecosystem restoration. Satellites, drones, and aerial imaging provide continuous data on land cover, vegetation health, soil moisture, and water dynamics. Multispectral and hyperspectral sensors allow detailed assessments of ecosystem conditions, detecting stress in vegetation or tracking sedimentation in rivers and wetlands. High-resolution imagery enables restoration practitioners to map degraded areas, prioritize interventions, and track changes over time. By covering vast and often inaccessible regions, remote sensing provides the spatial and temporal information needed for large-scale restoration planning.

AI enhances the value of remote sensing by automating data analysis and revealing patterns that would otherwise remain hidden. Machine learning algorithms process enormous datasets to classify land cover, predict ecosystem responses, and detect trends. For example, AI can differentiate between natural regeneration and planted forests, or distinguish invasive species from native vegetation in complex landscapes. Predictive models powered by AI help forecast how ecosystems will respond to interventions under different climate and land-use scenarios. These insights allow decision-makers to design restoration strategies that are adaptive, cost-effective, and resilient to future uncertainties.

GIS are another critical digital tool. GIS integrates spatial data from multiple sources—remote sensing, field surveys, and socio-economic datasets—into a single platform for analysis and visualization. Restoration practitioners use GIS to map ecosystem services, model hydrological flows, and identify priority areas for intervention. Scenario planning tools within GIS allow stakeholders to explore trade-offs, such as balancing agricultural expansion with forest restoration. By combining ecological, economic, and social data, GIS supports integrated approaches that align restoration with broader land management and development goals.

Drones are becoming indispensable for ecosystem restoration. They provide high-resolution imagery at relatively low cost and can access areas that are difficult or dangerous to reach. Beyond monitoring, drones are increasingly used in active restoration, such as dispersing seeds across degraded lands or planting seedlings with precision. Equipped with AI-driven navigation systems, drones can operate autonomously, covering large areas quickly and efficiently. This accelerates reforestation and vegetation recovery while reducing labor costs. The ability of drones to collect frequent and detailed data also enhances adaptive management, enabling rapid adjustments to restoration practices.

Digital platforms for data sharing and collaboration are facilitating more inclusive and transparent restoration processes. Open-source platforms provide access to satellite imagery, climate projections, and restoration tools for governments, researchers, and communities. Mobile applications enable citizen scientists and local stakeholders to contribute field data, such as species observations or land-use changes. These platforms democratize access to information, enhance transparency, and foster community engagement. They also allow practitioners to track global progress toward restoration targets, such as those under the UN Decade on Ecosystem Restoration.

Modeling and simulation tools supported by AI are reshaping how restoration outcomes are planned. Dynamic models simulate ecological processes such as succession, nutrient cycling, or hydrological flows under various management strategies. AI enhances these models by incorporating large datasets and improving predictive accuracy. For example, models can predict how reforesting a watershed will affect water availability or how coral reef restoration may alter fisheries productivity. By simulating multiple scenarios, these tools reduce uncertainty and help stakeholders make informed choices that balance ecological and socio-economic objectives.

Digital twins are an emerging technology with significant potential for restoration. A digital twin is a virtual replica of an ecosystem that integrates real-time monitoring data, historical records, and predictive models. These systems allow continuous assessment of ecological conditions and forecast how ecosystems will respond to interventions. Digital twins make it possible to test restoration strategies virtually before implementing them on the ground, reducing risks and costs. They also provide a platform for engaging stakeholders, visualizing potential outcomes, and supporting adaptive management over the long term.

AI and digital tools are also enhancing financial and governance mechanisms for restoration. Automated monitoring reduces the cost and complexity of verifying restoration outcomes, which is crucial for financing mechanisms such as carbon credits or biodiversity offsets. Blockchain technology, combined with AI, is being explored to ensure transparency in financial flows and ecological performance, reducing risks of fraud or misreporting. These innovations build trust among investors, governments, and communities, unlocking greater financial support for restoration projects.

Despite their promise, digital tools and AI are not without challenges. Access to technology and expertise remains uneven, particularly in developing countries. High costs, data privacy concerns, and technical limitations may also restrict widespread use. There is a risk that reliance on technology could overshadow local knowledge and community participation, which are essential for sustainable restoration. To maximize benefits, digital tools must be integrated with participatory approaches that respect traditional knowledge and local contexts. Capacity building, technology transfer, and inclusive governance are vital to ensure that digital innovation supports equitable and effective restoration.

Digital tools, AI, and remote sensing are revolutionizing ecosystem restoration by making it more data-driven, efficient, and scalable. From mapping and monitoring to predictive modeling and financial verification, these technologies provide the precision and speed needed to meet global restoration targets. By integrating digital innovation with local knowledge, participatory governance, and strong institutional frameworks, societies can harness these tools to accelerate ecological recovery and secure the natural systems on which human well-being depends.

Monitoring and Evaluation of Restoration Outcomes

Monitoring and evaluation (M&E) of restoration outcomes are critical for ensuring that efforts to repair degraded ecosystems achieve their intended goals. Restoration is a long-term process, often taking years or decades before full benefits are realized, making systematic tracking essential for adaptive management, accountability, and learning. Effective M&E frameworks measure ecological recovery, social and economic benefits, and governance outcomes, providing evidence to guide future interventions. Without robust monitoring, restoration risks becoming symbolic rather than transformative, with little understanding of whether resources are generating meaningful ecological and societal gains.

At the heart of M&E is the need to define clear objectives and indicators. Restoration projects often aim to restore biodiversity, ecosystem functions, and services such as water purification, carbon sequestration, or soil fertility. Indicators must therefore reflect both ecological and socio-economic dimensions. Ecological indicators might include species richness, vegetation cover, soil organic matter, or water quality. Socio-economic indicators could track livelihood improvements, job creation, or community participation. Selecting appropriate indicators ensures that M&E captures the multifaceted nature of restoration outcomes rather than focusing narrowly on a single metric.

Baseline assessments provide the foundation for monitoring. Understanding the initial condition of an ecosystem is necessary to measure progress and attribute changes to restoration actions. Baselines typically include ecological surveys, remote sensing imagery, and community assessments. In degraded areas where historical data are lacking, reference sites or models may be used to establish benchmarks. Establishing accurate baselines allows practitioners to set realistic goals and measure progress against a clear starting point.

Ecological monitoring techniques vary depending on the ecosystem and restoration objectives. Field surveys remain essential for collecting data on vegetation, soils, hydrology, and wildlife. Sampling plots, transects, and biodiversity inventories provide detailed insights into ecosystem changes. Remote sensing technologies complement field surveys by offering large-scale, repeatable data on land cover, vegetation health, and hydrological dynamics. Advances in eDNA and acoustic monitoring further enhance the ability to detect species presence and track biodiversity trends with minimal disturbance. By combining fieldwork with technology, practitioners can create comprehensive monitoring systems that capture both fine-scale and landscape-level changes.

Evaluation goes beyond tracking indicators to assess whether restoration is meeting its intended goals. This involves comparing observed outcomes with targets, assessing trade-offs, and considering unintended consequences. For example, a reforestation project may increase tree cover but reduce water availability if inappropriate species are used. Evaluation frameworks help identify such issues and allow practitioners to adjust strategies. Adaptive management, where monitoring results inform adjustments in practices, is central to ensuring that restoration is dynamic and responsive to changing conditions.

Socio-economic monitoring is equally important. Restoration affects communities, livelihoods, and equity, making it essential to assess human dimensions. Indicators might include household income, food security, or perceptions of well-being linked to restoration activities. Participatory monitoring, where communities contribute to data collection and evaluation, enhances inclusivity and ensures that local knowledge and values are integrated. It also fosters ownership, building long-term support for restoration. Evaluating socio-economic outcomes ensures that restoration contributes not only to ecosystems but also to human resilience and development.

Governance and institutional aspects also require monitoring. Effective restoration depends on transparent decision-making, stakeholder engagement, and clear land tenure. M&E frameworks should track governance processes, such as levels of community participation, conflict resolution, or alignment with policies and regulations. Strong governance indicators provide insights into the sustainability of restoration beyond ecological outcomes, ensuring that restored ecosystems are managed fairly and effectively over time.

Reporting and communication are critical elements of M&E. Results must be communicated clearly to stakeholders, including governments, funders, communities, and the public. Transparent reporting builds trust, attracts continued investment, and strengthens accountability. Global platforms, such as those supporting the UN Decade on Ecosystem Restoration, encourage countries and organizations to share data, fostering learning and collaboration. Clear communication also helps highlight the co-benefits of restoration, from climate mitigation to improved livelihoods, reinforcing the value of continued investment.

Innovations in digital tools are transforming monitoring and evaluation. Cloud-based platforms allow real-time data collection, storage, and analysis. Mobile applications enable field teams and citizen scientists to record observations directly, while AI-driven analytics enhance the interpretation of complex datasets. Dashboards and visualization tools make monitoring results accessible to diverse stakeholders, from policymakers to local communities. These innovations increase efficiency, reduce costs, and expand participation, making M&E more inclusive and scalable.

Challenges remain in implementing effective M&E. Long-term monitoring requires sustained funding, yet restoration projects often face short-term financial cycles. Data gaps, particularly in remote or resource-limited regions, limit the ability to track progress comprehensively. Ensuring comparability across projects and regions can also be difficult due to varying methodologies and indicators. Addressing these challenges requires investment in capacity building, standardized frameworks, and long-term financial mechanisms that support ongoing monitoring beyond project lifespans.

Monitoring and evaluation of restoration outcomes provide the evidence base needed to improve effectiveness, ensure accountability, and demonstrate the value of investment in ecosystems. By tracking ecological, socio-economic, and governance dimensions, M&E captures the full scope of restoration impacts. Advances in technology and participatory approaches are making monitoring more accurate, efficient, and inclusive. While challenges remain, robust M&E ensures that restoration delivers real, lasting benefits for both people and nature, guiding efforts toward a sustainable and resilient future.

Scaling Up Restoration Through Innovation

Ecosystem restoration at the scale required to address global challenges cannot rely solely on traditional approaches. While local initiatives are important, they are often fragmented and limited in scope. Scaling up restoration requires innovation across science, technology, governance, and finance. Innovative methods allow projects to move from isolated successes to systemic transformations, where restoration becomes embedded in economic systems, development planning, and community livelihoods. By harnessing new ideas and practices, societies can accelerate the pace, broaden the reach, and increase the impact of restoration efforts.

One key area of innovation is in ecological science and practice. Traditional restoration methods, such as planting trees or rehabilitating wetlands, are being enhanced with improved ecological understanding. Assisted natural regeneration, for example, leverages existing ecological processes to accelerate recovery at lower cost. Innovations in seed technologies, including drought-tolerant and pest-resistant varieties, increase survival rates in challenging environments. Genetic research is helping to identify species and populations that are more resilient to climate change, enabling restoration that is adaptive and forward-looking. These advances improve effectiveness while making restoration more sustainable over the long term.

Technological innovation is also reshaping restoration. Remote sensing, drones, and artificial intelligence are revolutionizing how degraded areas are identified, monitored, and managed. Drones can disperse millions of seeds in hours, covering large areas more quickly and cheaply than manual planting. AI analyzes satellite data to detect changes in vegetation cover, predict ecosystem responses, and optimize intervention strategies. Digital twins, or virtual models of ecosystems, allow practitioners to simulate restoration scenarios before implementation. These tools increase efficiency, reduce costs, and enhance accountability, making large-scale restoration more feasible and transparent.

Financial innovation is crucial for scaling up restoration. Traditional funding sources are insufficient, but new instruments such as green bonds, sustainability-linked loans, and carbon credits are mobilizing capital at scale. Payment for ecosystem services schemes create ongoing revenue streams for landowners and communities, linking restoration outcomes with financial rewards. Blended finance mechanisms, where public funds reduce risks for private investors, unlock investment in restoration projects that would otherwise be deemed too risky. Innovative insurance models, such as mangrove or reef insurance, further connect financial resilience with ecological resilience. By diversifying funding sources and linking restoration to markets, financial innovation expands resources for scaling.

Social innovation plays a central role in scaling restoration. Community-led initiatives, participatory governance, and inclusive approaches ensure that restoration is grounded in local realities and benefits those most directly affected. Innovative social arrangements, such as cooperatives or community-based enterprises, allow restoration to contribute directly to livelihoods. Education and capacity building strengthen local expertise, enabling communities to take ownership of restoration projects. Social media and digital platforms amplify engagement, connecting local efforts to global movements and fostering accountability. Scaling restoration requires that innovation not only improves ecological outcomes but also strengthens equity and inclusion.

Policy and governance innovations provide the enabling environment for large-scale restoration. Traditional top-down policies are being complemented by multi-level governance frameworks that integrate local, national, and international actors. Policy innovations include embedding restoration targets in climate commitments, land-use planning, and development strategies. Market-based instruments, regulatory incentives, and voluntary standards create alignment between economic activity and restoration goals. International frameworks, such as the UN Decade on Ecosystem Restoration, provide platforms for knowledge sharing and coordination, helping to align efforts across borders and sectors. By fostering coherent and adaptive governance, policy innovation helps scale restoration beyond individual projects.

Innovation is also evident in cross-sectoral integration. Restoration is increasingly linked with agriculture, energy, water, and urban development, creating synergies across sectors. Agroforestry systems restore ecosystems while increasing food production and farmer incomes. Green infrastructure integrates ecological restoration into urban planning, reducing flooding while enhancing urban biodiversity. Watershed restoration supports water security for agriculture, industry, and households. By embedding restoration within multiple sectors, innovation ensures that ecological recovery contributes directly to economic and social priorities, increasing incentives for large-scale adoption.

Global collaboration and knowledge exchange further enable scaling through innovation. Networks of practitioners, researchers, and policymakers share lessons learned, best practices, and technological advances. Open-source platforms provide access to data, methodologies, and monitoring tools, lowering barriers for participation. Partnerships between governments, businesses, and civil society create opportunities to pool resources and expertise. These collaborative innovations ensure that successful approaches are not confined to one context but are adapted and replicated across diverse ecosystems and regions.

Scaling up restoration through innovation requires overcoming challenges as well. Access to technology, finance, and knowledge is often unequal, particularly for developing countries and marginalized communities. Ensuring that innovations are inclusive, affordable, and context-appropriate is essential for equitable scaling. Safeguards are needed to prevent unintended consequences, such as promoting monocultures or excluding traditional knowledge. Strong governance and accountability mechanisms ensure that innovations deliver real ecological and social benefits rather than becoming vehicles for greenwashing. Addressing these challenges strengthens the credibility and effectiveness of scaling efforts.

Restoration at scale demands a shift from incremental projects to transformative systems. Innovation across ecological science, technology, finance, social engagement, and governance provides the means to achieve this shift. By accelerating recovery, mobilizing resources, and embedding restoration into broader development processes, innovation transforms restoration into a global movement capable of reversing decades of degradation. Scaling up through innovation ensures that restoration is not only larger in scope but also smarter, more inclusive, and more resilient, paving the way for ecosystems and societies to thrive together.

Chapter 9: Future Directions in Ecosystem Restoration

The future of ecosystem restoration will be defined by how societies respond to accelerating climate change, biodiversity loss, and resource pressures. By 2050, restoration must be scaled, integrated, and adaptive, linking ecological recovery with development, equity, and innovation. Advances in science, technology, and governance will shape new approaches, while financing tools and global cooperation expand opportunities for impact. Restoration will increasingly serve as a foundation for climate adaptation, sustainable economies, and social resilience. This chapter examines pathways to embed restoration within long-term strategies, ensuring it becomes a transformative force for creating thriving ecosystems and resilient human communities.

Building Resilience to Climate Change

Ecosystem restoration is one of the most effective strategies for building resilience to climate change. As climate impacts intensify through rising temperatures, shifting rainfall patterns, sea-level rise, and increased frequency of extreme weather events, the capacity of societies to adapt depends heavily on the health of ecosystems. Restored ecosystems act as natural buffers, reduce vulnerability, and provide critical resources that support livelihoods and economies under changing conditions. Integrating resilience into restoration ensures that ecosystems not only recover from past degradation but also remain functional in a future shaped by climate uncertainty.

Forests play a central role in climate resilience. Healthy and restored forests stabilize soils, regulate water cycles, and provide shade and cooling in both rural and urban areas. They also reduce disaster risks by preventing landslides and floods during heavy rains. Climate-resilient forest restoration incorporates diverse, native species that can adapt to changing conditions, rather than monocultures that are more vulnerable to pests, disease, and climatic extremes. Mixed-species plantings and assisted natural regeneration strengthen forest resilience while supporting biodiversity and local communities that depend on forest resources.

Wetlands and coastal ecosystems also provide vital climate resilience. Restored wetlands act as natural sponges, absorbing floodwaters, filtering pollutants, and maintaining water supplies during droughts. Coastal ecosystems such as mangroves, seagrasses, and coral reefs shield shorelines from storm surges and erosion. By reducing the need for costly engineered defenses, these ecosystems protect vulnerable coastal communities while sustaining fisheries and tourism. Restoration in these systems must consider climate impacts, such as sea-level rise and ocean acidification, ensuring that ecosystems remain robust as conditions evolve.

Agricultural landscapes are particularly vulnerable to climate change, making restoration critical for food security and resilience. Practices such as regenerative agriculture, agroforestry, and soil restoration improve the ability of farming systems to withstand drought, floods, and heat stress. Restored soils with higher organic matter retain more water and nutrients, reducing crop failure risks. Agroforestry systems integrate trees into farmland, providing shade, improving microclimates, and diversifying farmer incomes. By embedding restoration into agriculture, societies reduce vulnerability while supporting sustainable food production.

Water security is another dimension where restoration builds resilience. Healthy watersheds regulate flows, recharge aquifers, and improve water quality, buffering against both drought and flooding. River and stream restoration reduces erosion, stabilizes banks, and enhances water storage. These interventions ensure reliable water supplies for households, agriculture, and industry under variable climatic conditions. As climate change intensifies water stress globally, watershed and freshwater restoration become essential strategies for sustaining economies and reducing conflict over scarce resources.

Urban areas also benefit from restoration as a resilience strategy. Green infrastructure—including urban forests, parks, wetlands, and permeable surfaces—reduces urban heat islands, manages stormwater, and improves air quality. Restored urban ecosystems provide cooling during heatwaves, absorb rainfall during intense storms, and improve the well-being of residents. By embedding ecosystem restoration into urban planning, cities can adapt to climate risks while creating healthier and more livable environments. These approaches also contribute to social resilience by providing equitable access to green spaces and reducing environmental inequalities.

Resilience requires adaptive approaches in restoration planning and implementation. Climate projections must inform species selection, landscape design, and management practices to ensure ecosystems remain functional under future conditions. This may involve assisted migration, where species are introduced into areas expected to become suitable in the future, or the use of drought- and salt-tolerant species in areas facing intensified stress. Flexible and adaptive management systems enable restoration to respond to new information and changing conditions over time.

Community involvement is vital to building climate resilience through restoration. Local communities often bear the brunt of climate impacts and possess valuable knowledge about coping strategies. Participatory restoration ensures that interventions align with local needs and priorities while building capacity for long-term stewardship. When communities see tangible benefits—such as improved water access, reduced disaster risks, or enhanced livelihoods—they are more likely to support and sustain restoration. This integration of ecological and social resilience strengthens the adaptive capacity of societies as a whole.

Financing mechanisms must also align restoration with climate resilience goals. Climate finance, including adaptation funds and carbon markets, provides opportunities to scale restoration that delivers both mitigation and adaptation benefits. Investments in nature-based solutions are increasingly recognized as cost-effective strategies for reducing climate risks while supporting development.

By framing restoration as both an environmental and adaptation investment, societies can attract greater funding and mainstream resilience into development planning.

Building resilience to climate change through restoration highlights the dual role of ecosystems in mitigating risks and providing resources for adaptation. Forests, wetlands, agricultural systems, watersheds, and urban environments all benefit from restoration that reduces vulnerability and supports sustainable livelihoods. Adaptive, inclusive, and well-financed restoration ensures that ecosystems remain functional under uncertain futures. By embedding resilience in restoration strategies, societies create natural safety nets that protect people, economies, and biodiversity in the face of a changing climate.

Ecosystem Restoration and the Bioeconomy

The bioeconomy, which encompasses the sustainable use of biological resources for food, materials, energy, and services, is increasingly seen as a pathway to reconcile economic growth with environmental sustainability. At its core, the bioeconomy relies on healthy ecosystems that provide renewable resources and ecosystem services. Ecosystem restoration is therefore fundamental to unlocking the potential of the bioeconomy. By repairing degraded landscapes, forests, soils, wetlands, and marine systems, restoration ensures a continuous supply of biomass while safeguarding the ecological foundations on which the bioeconomy depends.

Restoration strengthens the resource base for the bioeconomy by improving productivity and resilience in terrestrial and aquatic ecosystems. Degraded soils, for instance, limit crop yields and restrict opportunities for sustainable agriculture. Through practices such as regenerative agriculture, agroforestry, and soil enrichment, restoration enhances soil fertility, increases water retention, and promotes biodiversity, all of which improve the quality and quantity of biomass. In forests, restoration increases the availability of timber, non-timber forest products, and genetic resources, providing raw materials for industries ranging from construction to pharmaceuticals. In marine and coastal systems, restoring habitats such as mangroves, seagrasses, and coral reefs supports fisheries, aquaculture, and bio-based industries dependent on healthy marine ecosystems.

Circularity is a defining feature of the bioeconomy, and ecosystem restoration supports this principle by closing resource loops. Restored ecosystems recycle nutrients, store carbon, and regulate hydrological cycles, reducing the need for external inputs and lowering environmental impacts. For example, restored wetlands act as natural water treatment systems, reducing reliance on costly engineered solutions. Agroecological practices restore soil and biodiversity, allowing agriculture to function more like a closed-loop system. By embedding restoration into the bioeconomy, societies reduce waste, increase efficiency, and ensure that resource use remains within ecological limits.

The bioeconomy is also closely linked to climate action, and restoration strengthens this connection. Restored ecosystems sequester carbon in biomass and soils, contributing to climate mitigation while supporting adaptation through increased resilience. Bio-based industries can reduce reliance on fossil fuels by producing renewable energy, bioplastics, and bio-based chemicals. However, scaling the bioeconomy requires ensuring that biomass sourcing is sustainable. Restoration plays a critical role here by expanding the resource base without further degrading ecosystems. By combining restoration with sustainable harvesting, societies can grow the bioeconomy while reducing pressure on natural systems.

Innovation in the bioeconomy depends heavily on restored ecosystems. Genetic diversity found in restored landscapes and seascapes provides the raw material for biotechnology, pharmaceuticals, and new materials. Biodiversity is a source of innovation, offering potential solutions to health, energy, and industrial challenges. Restoring degraded ecosystems not only conserves genetic diversity but also creates opportunities for bio-discovery, where new products and processes are developed from nature's resources. This dynamic highlights the interdependence of restoration and innovation within the bioeconomy.

Ecosystem restoration also supports rural development and inclusive growth within the bioeconomy. Many restoration activities—such as tree planting, soil rehabilitation, or community-based fisheries management—create jobs and strengthen local livelihoods. These activities provide opportunities for smallholders, indigenous peoples, and local communities to participate in the bioeconomy by producing biomass, managing resources, or engaging in eco-enterprises. Restoration ensures that participation is not limited to large industrial players but includes local actors who benefit from resource stewardship. By creating equitable opportunities, restoration helps build a more inclusive bioeconomy that addresses both environmental and social goals.

Policy frameworks are central to linking restoration with the bioeconomy. Governments can incentivize restoration through subsidies, tax breaks, and payment for ecosystem services, encouraging landowners and businesses to invest in sustainable practices. Policies that promote sustainable biomass sourcing, biodiversity conservation, and climate commitments align restoration with bioeconomic strategies. International frameworks, such as the EU Bioeconomy Strategy or the UN Decade on Ecosystem Restoration, provide platforms for integrating ecological and economic objectives. By embedding restoration into policy, governments ensure that the bioeconomy is grounded in long-term ecological sustainability.

Financing mechanisms further connect restoration with the bioeconomy. Green bonds, carbon markets, and impact investments channel capital toward projects that deliver both ecological and economic benefits. For example, investors may support reforestation initiatives that provide biomass for sustainable industries while generating carbon credits. Blended finance models de-risk investments in restoration, making them attractive to private sector actors. By mobilizing financial flows, innovative instruments expand the capacity of restoration to support bioeconomic development.

Challenges remain in fully aligning ecosystem restoration with the bioeconomy. Unsustainable biomass production, land-use conflicts, and overexploitation of resources risk undermining both ecological and economic goals. Restoration must be guided by principles of sustainability, inclusivity, and resilience to avoid repeating patterns of degradation. Monitoring and evaluation are critical to ensuring that restoration supports ecological integrity while enabling bioeconomic growth. Safeguards, clear standards, and participatory governance ensure that restoration contributes positively to ecosystems and communities.

Ecosystem restoration and the bioeconomy are mutually reinforcing. Restoration rebuilds the ecological foundations that supply biomass, genetic diversity, and ecosystem services, while the bioeconomy provides the economic rationale and financial flows needed to sustain restoration at scale. Together, they create opportunities for innovation, inclusive development, and climate resilience. By embedding restoration into the bioeconomy, societies can transform how resources are produced, consumed, and valued, ensuring that economic growth supports, rather than undermines, the health of the planet.

Mainstreaming Restoration into Development Planning

Integrating ecosystem restoration into development planning is critical for achieving long-term sustainability, resilience, and inclusive growth. Development planning traditionally prioritizes economic growth, infrastructure expansion, and social welfare, often overlooking the ecological foundations that underpin these goals. As ecosystems degrade and climate risks intensify, it is increasingly evident that restoration must be treated not as a separate environmental objective but as a core component of national, regional, and local planning. Mainstreaming restoration ensures that development strategies are ecologically sound, socially just, and resilient to future uncertainties.

A central reason for mainstreaming restoration into development planning is the recognition of ecosystems as natural capital. Forests, soils, wetlands, rivers, and coastal ecosystems provide services such as water regulation, carbon storage, disaster risk reduction, and biodiversity conservation, all of which directly support development objectives. When ecosystems are degraded, the costs of delivering these services rise, often requiring expensive engineered substitutes. By embedding restoration into planning, governments and institutions protect and enhance natural capital, ensuring that economic growth does not come at the expense of ecological stability.

Mainstreaming requires aligning restoration with national development priorities. Many countries pursue objectives such as food security, poverty reduction, climate adaptation, and energy access, all of which depend on healthy ecosystems. Restored soils and watersheds enhance agricultural productivity, supporting food security. Forest restoration contributes to rural employment and income, reducing poverty. Mangrove and wetland restoration protect coastal infrastructure from flooding, strengthening climate adaptation. By linking restoration outcomes to core development goals, policymakers create synergies that make restoration a development priority rather than an environmental add-on.

Sectoral integration is a key step in mainstreaming restoration. Development planning typically involves multiple sectors, including agriculture, water, energy, transport, and urban development. Each of these sectors both affects and depends on ecosystems. For instance, agricultural policies that promote sustainable practices and soil restoration directly enhance food systems, while energy policies that protect watersheds safeguard hydropower potential. Integrating restoration across sectors reduces trade-offs, promotes efficiency, and ensures that development is pursued within ecological limits. Multi-sectoral coordination mechanisms and cross-ministerial platforms can facilitate this integration.

Urban development planning offers a clear opportunity to embed restoration. Rapid urbanization often leads to the loss of natural habitats, increased pollution, and higher vulnerability to climate risks. By incorporating green infrastructure, urban forests, and wetland restoration into city planning, municipalities can reduce flood risks, improve air quality, and create healthier living environments. Mainstreaming restoration in urban contexts also enhances social inclusion, providing equitable access to green spaces and improving the quality of life for marginalized communities. Cities that integrate restoration into planning not only address environmental challenges but also become more resilient, competitive, and livable.

National and international policy frameworks provide important platforms for mainstreaming restoration. Commitments under the Paris Agreement, the Convention on Biological Diversity, and the Sustainable Development Goals all emphasize restoration as a strategy for climate, biodiversity, and development. NDCs and National Biodiversity Strategies and Action Plans (NBSAPs) increasingly include restoration targets. Development plans that align with these frameworks ensure coherence between national strategies and global commitments. This alignment also facilitates access to international funding and technical support for restoration activities.

Economic planning tools are essential for mainstreaming restoration. Cost-benefit analyses, natural capital accounting, and ecosystem service valuation provide evidence for the economic rationale of restoration. These tools demonstrate that investments in restoration yield long-term benefits by reducing disaster risks, increasing productivity, and avoiding costly environmental damage. By incorporating ecosystem values into economic planning, governments and businesses can make more informed decisions that recognize restoration as an investment rather than a cost. Integrating restoration into macroeconomic frameworks further strengthens its position within national budgets and development strategies.

Financing mechanisms must also support mainstreaming. Development banks, climate funds, and private investors are increasingly recognizing the role of restoration in achieving sustainable development. Embedding restoration in development planning ensures that financing for infrastructure, agriculture, or energy projects also supports ecological recovery. Blended finance arrangements, green bonds, and payment for ecosystem services can be structured within development programs, linking financial flows directly to restoration outcomes. By aligning financial systems with ecological objectives, mainstreaming ensures that restoration is adequately funded and sustainable.

Participation and governance are central to embedding restoration into development planning. Communities, indigenous peoples, and local organizations play vital roles in implementing and sustaining restoration. Participatory planning processes ensure that restoration aligns with local needs and knowledge, while also enhancing equity and social legitimacy. Governance frameworks that integrate multiple stakeholders strengthen accountability, reduce conflicts, and promote shared responsibility for restoration outcomes. Inclusive governance ensures that mainstreaming does not impose top-down solutions but reflects diverse perspectives and priorities.

Monitoring and evaluation systems are necessary for ensuring that mainstreaming delivers results. Development planning often involves long time horizons, and restoration outcomes may take decades to fully emerge. Integrating ecological, social, and economic indicators into development monitoring systems ensures that progress is tracked holistically. Transparent reporting and adaptive management allow governments and stakeholders to adjust strategies as conditions change. By embedding monitoring into planning cycles, mainstreaming ensures that restoration is a continuous, dynamic process.

Mainstreaming restoration into development planning transforms how societies approach growth and sustainability. It shifts restoration from being a discrete environmental initiative to a foundational strategy that underpins economic, social, and ecological resilience. By aligning restoration with national priorities, integrating it across sectors, embedding it in policy and finance, and ensuring inclusive governance, development planning can deliver outcomes that are both prosperous and sustainable. In doing so, restoration becomes a driver of long-term resilience, supporting the intertwined goals of human well-being and planetary health.

Visioning a Restored Planet by 2050

By 2050, the vision of a restored planet is one where ecosystems across terrestrial, freshwater, marine, and urban landscapes are no longer seen as depleted resources but as thriving foundations of life and prosperity. Restoration efforts carried out at scale over the next three decades could reverse centuries of degradation, creating a future in which natural capital is valued alongside human, social, and financial capital. The world of 2050 would be defined by healthier ecosystems, resilient societies, and economies that operate in harmony with ecological limits.

Forests would once again cover vast areas of the planet, functioning as carbon sinks, biodiversity havens, and sources of livelihood for millions. Restoration would have reversed deforestation trends, expanded natural forests, and diversified tree species to create landscapes resilient to climate change. Reforested and regenerated areas would support sustainable forestry, agroforestry, and ecotourism industries, aligning ecological goals with economic development. Forest-dependent communities would benefit from secure land rights, improved livelihoods, and active participation in restoration governance.

Freshwater systems, once degraded by pollution, over-extraction, and fragmentation, would flow more freely and support abundant biodiversity. Rivers would be reconnected through dam removals or bypass channels, allowing fish migrations to thrive once again. Wetlands, lakes, and reservoirs restored by 2050 would function as critical buffers against floods and droughts, while also recharging aquifers and filtering pollutants. Watershed management practices would ensure reliable water supplies for agriculture, industry, and households, making water security a cornerstone of both climate resilience and human well-being.

Coastal and marine ecosystems would be revitalized as frontline defenses against climate change. Mangroves, salt marshes, and seagrass meadows would have expanded, reducing coastal erosion, sequestering carbon, and sustaining fisheries. Coral reef restoration, aided by technological advances, would allow reefs to adapt and recover from bleaching events, preserving biodiversity hotspots and supporting tourism and fishing livelihoods. Marine protected areas, combined with sustainable fisheries management, would ensure that oceans once again teem with life, supporting both biodiversity and food security.

In agricultural landscapes, degraded soils would have been restored through regenerative practices, enhancing productivity while reducing dependence on chemical inputs. By 2050, farming systems would integrate trees, crops, and livestock in ways that mimic natural ecosystems, increasing resilience to climate variability and diversifying farmer incomes. Restoration of grasslands and savannas would revive ecosystems critical for pollinators, wildlife, and pastoralist livelihoods. Agriculture and restoration would be seen not as opposing goals but as mutually reinforcing strategies for feeding the world sustainably.

Urban environments would be transformed into green, resilient, and inclusive spaces. Cities would be reimagined with extensive green infrastructure, including urban forests, green roofs, restored rivers, and wetlands integrated into design. These ecosystems would reduce heat islands, absorb stormwater, improve air quality, and enhance urban biodiversity. By 2050, urban residents would enjoy equitable access to nature, improving health, well-being, and social cohesion. Restoration embedded in urban planning would make cities more livable and better prepared for climate-related shocks.

Economically, restoration would be fully embedded within the global development agenda, forming a pillar of the bioeconomy. Restored ecosystems would provide renewable resources for industries, support sustainable energy generation, and sustain livelihoods through nature-based enterprises. Innovative financing mechanisms—green bonds, carbon markets, biodiversity credits, and blended finance—would channel billions of dollars annually into restoration. These financial systems would ensure that restoration is not dependent on short-term projects but supported as an investment in long-term sustainability and resilience.

Socially, restoration would have become a vehicle for justice and inclusion. Indigenous peoples and local communities would be recognized as stewards of ecosystems, with their knowledge systems integrated into restoration practices. Equitable benefit-sharing arrangements would ensure that those most dependent on ecosystems are also the primary beneficiaries of restoration gains. Restoration would strengthen social resilience, reduce inequality, and foster collaboration across borders and cultures.

Technological and scientific advances would play a central role in achieving this vision. AI, remote sensing, genetic research, and ecological engineering would provide tools for large-scale monitoring, predictive modeling, and adaptive management. Restoration would no longer be reactive but proactive, designed with future climate and ecological conditions in mind. Knowledge sharing through global platforms would ensure that lessons learned in one region inform efforts elsewhere, creating a culture of collaboration and innovation.

A restored planet by 2050 would embody a fundamental shift in how humanity views its relationship with nature. Ecosystems would no longer be seen as expendable backdrops to human activity but as living systems essential for survival and prosperity. Restoration would underpin climate stability, economic resilience, and human well-being, redefining development as something inseparable from ecological health. By weaving restoration into every sector—agriculture, energy, water, infrastructure, and urban planning—societies would create a future in which people and nature thrive together, securing a healthier, more resilient planet for generations to come.

Conclusion

Ecosystem restoration has emerged as one of the most important strategies for addressing the intertwined challenges of environmental degradation, climate change, and sustainable development. It is not only an ecological imperative but also a social, economic, and moral responsibility. Throughout this exploration, restoration has been presented as a means of healing damaged landscapes, waters, and seascapes while simultaneously securing the foundations of human well-being. The vision for restoration is ambitious, yet it is grounded in evidence that healthy ecosystems provide the services and resilience necessary for societies to flourish.

Restoration must be understood as more than just repairing the past; it is about shaping a sustainable future. By investing in restoration, societies are safeguarding biodiversity, sequestering carbon, enhancing food and water security, and building resilience to disasters. Each chapter of this book has highlighted how restoration intersects with forests, grasslands, rivers, wetlands, marine systems, cities, and governance structures. Taken together, these domains demonstrate that restoration is not a sectoral task but a cross-cutting approach that requires integration into every aspect of planning, policy, and practice.

The pathways to achieving restoration are diverse and context-specific. In some places, restoration involves reforestation or soil regeneration, while in others it means rehabilitating coral reefs or creating green urban spaces. Regardless of form, successful restoration depends on combining scientific knowledge, technological innovation, and local expertise. It also requires enabling governance structures, adequate financing, and strong community participation. Importantly, restoration is most effective when it is designed inclusively, ensuring that the rights and needs of indigenous peoples and local communities are recognized and respected.

Financing restoration remains a critical challenge but also a powerful opportunity. Public funds, private investment, innovative market-based tools, and blended finance models all have roles to play in scaling up action. By linking restoration to economic development and the bioeconomy, it becomes not merely a cost but an investment in prosperity and resilience. As businesses, investors, and governments increasingly recognize the economic value of ecosystems, financial flows for restoration are likely to expand, further embedding restoration within global development strategies.

The future of restoration is also inseparable from innovation. Advances in ecological engineering, digital tools, artificial intelligence, and remote sensing are revolutionizing how ecosystems are restored and monitored. These technologies improve efficiency, reduce costs, and make large-scale efforts more feasible. At the same time, innovation must remain grounded in ecological principles and respect for local knowledge, ensuring that technological solutions complement rather than replace the wisdom of communities and the dynamics of natural systems.

By 2050, it is possible to envision a world where ecosystems are healthier, societies are more resilient, and economies are aligned with ecological realities. Achieving this vision will require sustained commitment, adaptive management, and collaboration across scales—from local communities to international institutions. The restoration of ecosystems is not simply about repairing damage but about transforming the relationship between humanity and nature into one that is regenerative and balanced.

Restoration is a journey that requires patience, persistence, and creativity. It calls for a recognition that human well-being is inseparable from the health of the planet. As restoration continues to be mainstreamed into development planning, financed through innovative mechanisms, and guided by science and local wisdom, it offers a pathway toward a more resilient, inclusive, and sustainable future. Ecosystem restoration is not only possible; it is essential for securing the prosperity of both people and the natural world in the decades ahead.

www.ingramcontent.com/pod-product-compliance
Lightning Source LLC
Chambersburg PA
CBHW052137270326
41930CB00012B/2927